Major Washington's Pittsburgh

and the

Mission to Fort Le Boeuf

BRADY J. CRYTZER

THE
History
PRESS

Published by The History Press
Charleston, SC 29403
www.historypress.net

Cover images by artist John Buxton, www.buxtonart.com. Front cover is *Washington's Crossing, 1753*, and back cover includes *French Creek 1753*, *Half-King and Christopher Gist* and *Washington at the Point, 1753*.

First published 2011
Manufactured in the United States

ISBN 978.1.60949.046.1

Library of Congress Cataloging-in-Publication Data

Crytzer, Brady.
Major Washington's Pittsburgh and the mission to Fort Le Boeuf / Brady Crytzer.
p. cm.
Includes bibliographical references and index.
ISBN 978-1-60949-046-1
1. Washington's Expedition to the Ohio, 1st, 1753-1754. 2. Washington, George,
1732-1799--Military leadership. 3. United States--History--French and Indian War,
1755-1763--Causes. I. Title.
E312.23.C79 2011
973.2'6--dc22
2011004526

CONTENTS

ACKNOWLEDGEMENTS

Without the efforts of those mentioned here and the countless others who are not, this book, and my career as a historian, would not be possible. These acknowledgements are the least that I can present as an expression of gratitude, and I offer them humbly. To my mother and father, for their endless support; to my brother, Kent, and his wife, Amy, for their encouragement; to my nieces, Kendall and Emily, for keeping me on my toes; to my grandfather and grandmother, for their timeless advice; to my extended (and ever growing) family, for their warmth and hospitality; to my friend and colleague, Ali Wyrostek, for her faithful adherence to proper citation; to the faculty and staff of the Department of History at Slippery Rock University, for their time and efforts, critiques and confidence; and most of all to Jennifer, for her unconditional love and understanding.

Prologue
HISTORICAL IDENTITIES

DEFINING A LEGACY

In life, George Washington was steadfast, privileged and determined. In death, however, he is suffering an identity crisis.

Throughout his youth, Washington was an ambitious member of the Virginia planter class. Like most men of his age, he envisioned his future as infinitely promising, with multiple avenues to explore and no milestone that he could not reach. *Unlike* most men of his age, however, the young Washington had the financial resources and political capital to truly pursue success. While there is decidedly little evidence about his early life, there is little question about his character in his very public later years. Serving as the commanding officer of the American Continental Army and eventually as the first president of the United States, the aged yet graceful Washington was the picture of resolve. In his time, he was a shining beacon, believed to be the embodiment of the resilient spirit of the newly founded America.

Following his death in 1799, the nation to which he was ascribed as "Father" would soon jockey for a legitimate claim to his postmortem sentiments; it would divide itself in the process. For political candidates of the nineteenth century touting their military service, Washington would become a barometer of both commitment and sacrifice. For those running on a more even-handed platform, he was a benchmark.

A contemporary reproduction of a disappointed George Washington during his campaigns in western Pennsylvania. *Courtesy of the Senator John Heinz History Center.*

Washington's image of benevolence and dedication to his country would soon thereafter serve a very different purpose as the United States spiraled into the Civil War. Across the South, would-be Confederate legislatures revered Washington as a slave owner, as well as a Southern gentleman operating within his God-given rights to life, liberty and property. While young men from across Dixie raised arms against their own nation, images of Washington volunteering to protect his homeland from the tyrannical British only a century before fluttered through their minds.

With booming shots ringing out across a once peaceful countryside, Confederate soldiers everywhere heard only the footsteps of George Washington.

Gen'l Washington at Prayer (1848), a nineteenth-century image reminiscent of Christ in the garden of Gethsemane. Images like these were meant to display Washington's extraordinary piety. J. Balbie, New York, artist. *Courtesy of the Old Stone House Museum.*

About a decade later, while a beaten and battered America was attempting to heal itself from the self-inflicted sins it had committed in the name of freedom, the nation celebrated its 100th birthday. If George Washington wasn't on the lips of good citizens everywhere before that, he certainly was then. Centennial celebrations sprang up across the country in towns both north and south of the Mason-Dixon line, and an association with the Founding Fathers was worth its weight in gold. Taverns and inns from Alabama to Vermont found new life, and new fortunes, in being able to proudly boast that "George Washington was here." Truth in advertising was a liability that most wouldn't have bothered to concern themselves with.

The dawn of the twentieth century and its new affinity for "progressivism" began to adopt Washington as well, but this time with a new approach. Viewing Washington and his 1776 cohorts as social innovators, a full spectrum of interest groups from labor to liberalism adopted their "revolutionary" ideals as passages to their own sought-after equality.

A statue of Washington at Kennywood Park in West Mifflin, Pennsylvania. As in the nineteenth century, claiming that "George was here" was sure to garner profit and attention. *Courtesy of the author.*

The rest of the century was, well, academic. In short, Washington and his *perceived* values became an instrument, a political mechanism used to reach out to a specialized constituency in order to reach a common goal.

The Depression era of the 1930s saw a particular emphasis develop on the personal virtues of Washington. Popular culture highlighted his resilience during the cold winter nights at Valley Forge, along with his never-ending perseverance against a much larger, and better financed, British army during the American Revolution. At times when the country needed to endure, it did so atop the shoulders of George Washington. Those perceptions were maintained through the struggle and fury of World War II and redefined the "Father of Our Country" for an entirely new generation.

There are cyclical patterns to be seen when looking closely at our American society. The notions of equality—or, more appropriately, *inequality*—returned in the 1960s during the civil rights movement. This time, though, race and gender took center stage rather than the precedents and special interests of sixty years before. Like had happened a century earlier, George Washington was once again revealed to be a slave owner and an aristocratic pillar of high society. He was swiftly taken *off* the pedestal and promptly placed on trial.

Although he was far from public enemy number one, Marxists and liberals would rarely mention his name without first qualifying it by mentioning his less scrupulous activities and associations.

This evaluation brings us to today's America. It has been more than two hundred years since George Washington was interred at his estate at Mount Vernon, and his true identity remains the evenly placed banner in a proverbial game of political and popular tug of war. Thanks, in part, to the rise of countless Hollywood epics and cable television networks, George Washington has become a new favorite target of conspiracy theorists and opportunistic sensationalists. Suddenly it was more about ties to clandestine, secret societies than any particular defining characteristic.

Washington was certainly a Freemason, but he took over the world all by himself. The political climate of recent years will surely dictate a new interpretation of Washington. In the spring of 2009, sentiments of anti-incumbency and antiestablishment swept the nation in a movement known as the Tea Party. Nonviolent yet extraordinarily emotional protests swelled to a boiling point from sea to shining sea, and the American populace was put on notice. Members of all political parties joined hands, huddled together and expressed their discontent for measures that they believed were violations of their Constitutional rights.

George Washington was a true American, a patriot of the highest order; he stood once again for truth and justice—to no surprise, the Tea Party stood with him. Mailboxes and windshields in every state were soon flooded with pamphlets and leaflets opening with basic prompts such as, "What does it REALLY mean to be an American?" and, "Do you know YOUR rights?" Soon to follow were convenient, pocket-sized editions of the Declaration of Independence and the United States Constitution. There was no degree of certainty regarding how factual those solicitations really were, but there was one guarantee: for those who struggled to answer those thought-provoking questions and dared to read the literature in front of them, an image of George Washington was sure to be somewhere inside.

Patriotic fervor had swept the nation once again, and old George was more than happy to lace up his boots and march under its banner. It may soon be time that, when referencing Washington in text, we capitalize the "H" in "He."

This book is not intended to rewrite the history of Washington's life, nor is it meant to redefine who Washington really was or what he really did. It is merely an attempt to inform the reader of what steps he took to become the man he will always be remembered as. Many books, texts, docudramas and articles have attempted to answer the question: "Who *was* George Washington?"

Perhaps the question we should be asking is: "Who will George Washington be *next?*"

DEFINING A CITY

The city of Pittsburgh, Pennsylvania, has been defined as hardy, industrious and, most recently, innovative; its inhabitants have largely resided within its city limits for their entire lives. They would describe it as a wonderful place to start a family, and the families of those fortunate enough to have done so have probably done it for generations. "The lucky ones are born here," a resident would claim. "The smart ones stay here."

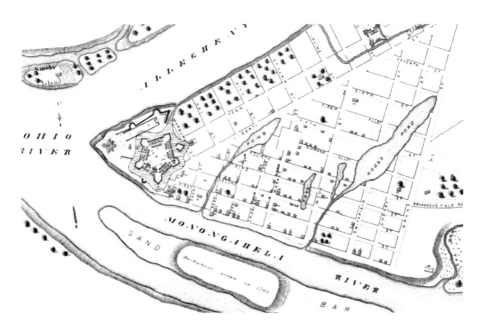

A representation of Pittsburgh in 1795. *From Thomas Cushing's* History of Allegheny County *(1889).*

Historical Identities

Pittsburgh's residents are some of the most charming, confidently modest people that the United States has to offer. Subsequently, it, too, is suffering from an identity crisis.

To understand how the city of Pittsburgh identifies itself, one must first gain a fundamental understanding of what the city of Pittsburgh is. Official statistics will claim that the relatively small metropolitan area is a mere 58.3 square miles, miniscule compared to 468.9 of New York City and still dwarfed when compared to the 135.0 of its cross-state neighbor, Philadelphia. Regarding population, numbers range from as low as 296,324 to 300,000. The average income of that group is estimated at about $32,000. By most standards, moving to the Pittsburgh area would be taking a financial loss. Jobs have steadily left the area since the second half of the twentieth century, and several of the previously mentioned figures have decreased in value.

Considering the figures just presented, one would be surprised to discover that, though it cannot be measured with any degree of accuracy, overall city morale has risen exponentially. Many unfamiliar with the Pittsburgh area would incorrectly credit that to its illustrious sports history. Known as the "City of Champions," Pittsburgh is home to a National Football League record six Lombardi trophies, three National Hockey League Stanley Cup titles and five World Series championships. It proudly supports a rich history of Negro League Baseball and a tradition of high school athletics that most would describe as sacred. One would not be faulted for believing that this sporting history alone is responsible for the generally sunny dispositions held by most of Pittsburgh's population.

Nevertheless, one would be negligent to simply dismiss this positive phenomenon via sporting excellence. A quick analysis of its recent baseball history though will reveal that, from March to October, the Pittsburgh Pirates have produced losing seasons in eighteen consecutive years. The question, then, begs again to be asked: How does a city in the midst of an economic downturn remain so upbeat, so willing to remain stationary and so anxious to declare itself victorious?

To answer that question may be deemed by some as futile, and no conclusion could be accepted as absolute. An exploration of the topic, though, will grant one a fuller, more complete perspective on the city of Pittsburgh and allow a more comprehensive understanding of its unique flavor. By examining the city at all levels, its endless quest for a singular historical identity will become apparent, as well as the obstacles that have prevented it from ever fully revealing itself.

To begin, few Pittsburghers actually reside within the geographic metropolitan limits of the city itself. In fact, most would take offense to being considered suburbanites or as any designation less worthy than a person who was raised in "Pittsburgh." It must be clarified that "Pittsburgh," in the manner that Pittsburghers use it, is actually a reference to the region surrounding the city center. The boundaries of this region are debated by its residents, and some who have relocated to different areas of the United States may even declare it as more of an ideology than as a temporal, geographic reality. But generally speaking, many would settle that "Pittsburgh" extends as far north as Erie, as far east as Harrisburg and as far south as Morgantown, West Virginia. There is, however, no debate that its western limit is promptly defined as the Pennsylvania-Ohio border.

The opening chapter of this text introduces the reader to a twenty-one-year-old George Washington as he stands candidly at the confluence of the Allegheny, Monongahela and Ohio Rivers. This triangular piece of land is a very specific geographical location that is held in reverence by the people of Pittsburgh city and Pittsburgh region alike. Its official administrative title is Point State Park, but it's more commonly known by its regional epithet: the

A glimpse into mid-nineteenth-century Pittsburgh. *From Robert Sears's* A New and Popular Pictorial Description of the United States *(1848)*.

Point. An afternoon spent at Point State Park will always be a pleasant one, and if privy to one of the many cultural festivities that take place there, visitors would consider their time quite enjoyable. Standing in stark contrast to the hurried metropolitan atmosphere close by, Point State Park is a jogger's haven, an ideal picnic destination and the area's most reliable setting for guaranteed meditative inspiration. The controlled rush of the iconic fountain, located on the far western tip of the park, affords visitors a unique opportunity to consider the events that took place there, as well as a spectacular view of the chaotic flow patterns that are the result of three massive waterways colliding.

An understanding of this piece of land's history serves as a useful case study for the conflicted history of the region as a whole, a quintessential microcosm of the "Steel City" itself. As will be seen in the chapters to follow, the location itself was held in high regard by the dominate European powers in the region, Great Britain and France, and a world war would break out to obtain control of it. During the French and Indian War, Fort Duquesne would quickly be established by the French, and it would just as quickly be abandoned when threatened by the forces of General John Forbes. Fort Pitt would be established in its place and would remain, in some form, for the next 250 years. Named after the British statesman William Pitt, the fort would give way to a bustling settlement that would also bear his name. Dubbed "Pittsburgh" by Scotsman John Forbes (pronounced "Pitts-boro," mirroring the Scottish city of Edinburgh, or "Edin-boro"), the town would give way to plots of farmland followed by a bustling urban community. So influential was Pitt's legacy on the region that his familial coat of arms would be adopted to grace the modern city's flag, and its bold black and gold coloration would soon become one of its most iconic pieces of symbolism.

As the eighteenth century came to a close, the city blossomed into a highly prized commercial destination by the emerging giants of American manufacturing. Its unique proximity to the Ohio River (which fed directly into the Mississippi) was instrumental in transporting finished goods to the heavily trafficked ports of southern cities, most notably Charleston and America's busiest port, New Orleans. So vital was the Ohio River that Meriwether Lewis and William Clark used the city as the launching point of their famous westward expedition.

Within fifty years, Pittsburgh was transformed from a military powerhouse to an emerging industrial metropolis.

For the next 120 years, the city would explode, courtesy of the Industrial Revolution. Americans everywhere marveled at the production capacity of Pittsburgh, its goods being used around the world as well. By 1857, there were more than nine hundred working factories employing more than ten thousand workers and producing more than $12 million per year. By 1910, the city had more than twenty-seven miles of usable harbor and produced more than $211 million. All the while, the plot known as the Point bore the scars and hardships of every dollar made. Lined with industrial rail and flooded with river traffic, the triangular strip of land once home to one of the nation's mightiest fortifications was now an instrument in the hands of some of the world's wealthiest industrialists.

With the rise of the industrial elite came the rise of organized resistance. Though the working class of Pittsburgh included laborers of Irish, Italian, Jewish, German, Slovak and African American descent, the multiethnic motion for rights was instituted under one united flag. Organized labor had

Part of a spectacular mural located in Pittsburgh's famous Station Square. *Courtesy of the author.*

found a home in the city of steel, and watershed moments like the Homestead Strike of 1892 helped to solidify the city's unwavering commitment to obtaining those rights at all costs. While the labor movement was not a direct innovation of the city of Pittsburgh, its outstanding dedication to the cause brought it to the forefront of its evolution in America. The city hand once again redefined itself, and it would do so again.

Like most cities of the time period, the efficiency and production of Pittsburgh's industrial enterprises would be crippled by the Great Depression of the 1930s. Like their countrymen, the people of Pittsburgh would endure, and at the beginning of the Second World War, a new chapter of the city's history would be written.

An integral part of President Franklin Delano Roosevelt's "Arsenal of Democracy," Pittsburgh led the charge in the manufacturing of precious steel, aluminum, machinery and munitions for the fighting men and women

Another part of a spectacular mural located in Pittsburgh's famous Station Square. *Courtesy of the author.*

of the Allied forces in Europe. From the start of the war until its conclusion in 1945, the factories that defined Pittsburgh for more than a century would produce about 95 million tons of steel. Despite this legacy, most Pittsburghers remain unaware of its integral contribution to the war effort. It is difficult to say with any degree of certainty where, why or how Pittsburgh lost track of its historical identity, but the reforms that followed in 1946 are considered by most to be the beginning.

Known pejoratively as the "Smoky City," the skies of Pittsburgh were blanketed by thick layers of unchecked industrial exhaust for nearly a century. Though environmentalism was just newly on the lips of ambitious reformers, it became apparent to all parties involved that the city required a change of image. Elected in 1945, Mayor David L. Lawrence, with the contribution of financial giant Richard K. Mellon, instituted the first of a series of urban renewal projects. Over the next thirty years, the trademark brownish-gray hue that characterized the skies over Pittsburgh cleared, and the demolition of long-standing industrial neighborhoods made way for revitalization projects such as the Civic Arena and Point State Park.

Pittsburgh had been beautified.

An astonishing trend would occur next. The memories that the city of Pittsburgh had tried so hard to forget—the days of sweltering fourteen-hour shifts in the now defunct mills of the city—were coming back. They were

A third part of a spectacular mural located in Pittsburgh's famous Station Square. The moniker "City of Champions" remains a great point of pride for the city and its people. *Courtesy of the author.*

As seen in Pittsburgh International Airport, these contemporary replicas place Franco Harris, the father of Steelers Country, and George Washington side by side. *Courtesy of the author.*

discussed in bars and barbershops, and the recollections shared were done in a thoughtful, not begrudging, manner.

The mechanism behind this new endearment for the industrial age is found at the end of World War II. With throngs of young veterans returning home, spirits were up, and for the first time, courtesy of the GI Bill, a college education was a realistic and attainable goal. With a wealth of opportunities ahead of them, most not involving factory labor, the veteran graduates of Pittsburgh paid homage to those who had scratched out a living in the mills a generation before—many of whom were their own parents.

Pittsburgh had become the "Steel City," and it was proud to be so.

What is Pittsburgh's true historical identity? Is it sporting excellence? Is it the long-standing legacy of industrialization? Or were both the result of shared, communal appreciation for the industrious spirit of the Pittsburgh region itself?

Major Washington's Pittsburgh

The Pittsburgh that George Washington knew was not different from that discussed previously. It was an unforgiving landscape where an unnatural commitment to success in the face of adversity was the only prerequisite. This book is not an attempt to give Pittsburgh a historical identity.

The cities of Boston and Philadelphia, despite their diverse pasts, universally agree to highlight their integral roles played during the American Revolution and early national period.

The true historical identity of Pittsburgh is as complex and rich as the city itself. Note Point State Park in the foreground. *Courtesy of the author.*

Pittsburgh cannot seem to come to terms with its past. It's a complicated question, but perhaps there is no singular identity readily available for the "Steel City." Perhaps Pittsburgh's history should be recalled without the presence of an agenda. Perhaps the best way to summarize or classify the city is not by restricting it to one aspect of its past but rather to allow it to unfold as a continuous narrative of ambition, confidence, versatility, restraint, resolve and frailty. George Washington's exploits in the Pittsburgh region could be argued as its most valuable historical legacy; this text will not defend that point. The following chapters simply offer that Washington's trials and triumphs are indicative of the region in which they occurred.

The man he would become, and the man America has since transformed him into, may not have existed without the hardships and successes that he experienced in the widespread region of western Pennsylvania—or, as the locals call it, Pittsburgh.

Chapter 1

AMBITION

The Commission of an Officer

APRIL 2010

With skyscrapers gleaming in the background, families and friends gathered joyously along the shores of the Allegheny, Monongahela and Ohio Rivers. Situated on a stretch of land encompassing about thirty-six acres, Point State Park has served as a beacon of civic pride for the city of Pittsburgh since its public opening in 1974. At the western edge—or, more appropriately, point—of the park sits a fountain famous for its central water jet that showers upward like a geyser to heights of 150 feet.

While the landmass was lined with industrial railway tracks for much of the late nineteenth and early twentieth century, it stands today as a lush monument to the storied history of the region known affectionately as the "Steel City." At the eastern edge of the park sits a one-of-a-kind museum chronicling the mighty fortress that once occupied this space. The Fort Pitt Museum houses some of America's most priceless artifacts from the eighteenth century and, since 1969, has delighted visitors from around the world. In August 2009, the Fort Pitt Museum was forced to close its doors. The timetable was set as "indefinitely."

Owned and operated by the Pennsylvania Historical and Museum Commission, and therefore a ward of the state, budget concerns tightened their cold grip on legislators in Harrisburg. With more pertinent issues looming, such as paying the earned wages of thousands of state employees, government officials were forced to curtail spending. The Fort Pitt Museum was soon joined in closing by the historic sites of Bushy Run Battlefield, the Joseph Priestley House and the Brandywine Battlefield.

Eight months later, colonial-era melodies of celebration drowned out the metropolitan "white noise" of the city that usually made them inaudible. On April 17, 2010, the Fort Pitt Museum reopened its doors to the public after being acquired by the delightfully hip John Heinz History Center. Reenactors, or "living historians" as they preferred to be called, gathered from across the country to commemorate the day that saved their beloved regional history. Those unaware of why the festivities were taking place simply wandered into the park to enjoy the unusually warm April weather. While some planned on only staying for a moment, many remained for the whole day. Fort Pitt belonged to Pittsburgh once more.

Sitting solemnly among the throngs of visitors was the Fort Pitt Blockhouse. The only remaining structure from the original earthen fortress, the blockhouse stands as a reminder. In its 250-year-old grace, the edifice is a testament to the fortitude of the timeless strength of the complex that, in the estimation of many, was the sole reason for the existence of modern-day Pittsburgh. The unassuming structure had seen the best and worst of the region's most prolific moments. It stood firm throughout numerous skirmishes with frontier natives; the dawn of a new, independent American nation; and an industrial revolution. It's all that remains of the original Fort Pitt.

More than 250 years before this public celebration, the landscape of Pittsburgh was very different. Dense forest replaced the benches and sidewalks of the park, and the rushing flood of the three rivers that surrounded it was flowing at a comparable whisper.

Also 250 years before the reopening of the Fort Pitt Museum, there stood on this ground an ambitious twenty-one-year-old named George Washington.

In his time, Great Britain and France would soon wage a seven-year world war for empire. By establishing oneself at the confluence of the Allegheny, Monongahela and Ohio Rivers, the weighty prospects of the New World were spoils to the victor. Europe's preeminent superpowers were set to do battle in unfamiliar territory for a prized parcel of land.

The world watched with bated breath to see who would control it.

November 23, 1753

With his canoe rolling gently on the shore of the icy Allegheny River, George Washington found himself deep in thought. He had always had a keen eye for inspecting the land around him. As a teenager, Washington had accompanied a surveying party on a mission to accurately chart the Blue Ridge Mountains in western Virginia. He had ventured into the wild before, but nothing like this.

Now, unlike his prior experiences, the subject of his deliberation was not the rolling landscape of the Shenandoah Valley but rather a small, snow-covered outcropping that forked two rivers into one. The landmass was not impressively large in his estimation, but it was uniquely suitable for establishing an outpost in the uncharted wilderness that was the Ohio Country. It was a risk and, for the unproven Washington, a second thought in the greater context of his larger mission. This unique piece of earth was known as the Forks of the Ohio, and it would soon be the center of a global conflict.

In his journal, Washington wrote, "A Fort at the Forks would be equally well situated on Ohio, and have the entire command of Monongahela, which runs up to our settlements and is extremely well designed for water carriage, as it is of a deep still nature; besides, a Fort at the Fork might be built at a much less expense, than at the other places."

Washington was determined to return to Virginia with the most useful of notes and, if possible, a recommendation for a new fort to sit beneath the British flag. As a student of geographic detail, the twenty-one-year-old took particular interest in the advantageous setting of the forks. Washington noted specifically that "[t]he land at the Point is 20 or 25 feet above the common surface of the water," with "well-timbered land all around it, very convenient for building." Washington describes the Monongahela River as "very rapid and swift running" and the Allegheny as "deep and still, without any perceptible fall." It is a stark contrast to the Forks of the Ohio as it runs in the twenty-first century.

In their present condition, the rivers that Washington spoke of are very different. While they were passable, in most parts, by foot in the eighteenth century, later industrial dredging and damming projects had made the three rivers mechanized "super highways" of barges and shipping vessels. With these alterations, the deep and still waters of the Allegheny quickly became the veritable lifeblood of western Pennsylvania's timber and steel industries.

Standing, however, where Washington stood, one can still obtain the same sense of wonder that the young Virginian felt. By keeping in mind the natural triangular design of Point State Park, the spider web of concrete footpaths and the large, spewing fountain can quickly be mentally erased and replaced with dense forest. The hills that surround it are in the same position that they were 250 years ago. The final and perhaps most challenging suspension of disbelief is substituting the powerful skyline of downtown Pittsburgh with lush, endless wilderness. After centuries have passed, the significance of this place is not lost on anyone.

Washington was well aware of the strategic importance of the forks, despite his lack of military training or experience. Surrounded on three sides by rivers, each of which was described by Washington as a quarter-mile across, assaults on any fortification built there would be directed only from

The French and British both had lofty ambitions for the Ohio Country. Station Square mural. *Courtesy of the author.*

the eastern side. As previously mentioned, the eastern portion of the forks expanded into a large, forested area suitable for ample hunting and logging to supply the potential outpost built there. The central location on the three waterways allowed goods and infantry to move north using the Allegheny, south courtesy of the Monongahela and west via the Ohio. If the British empire was going to establish itself as supreme in the wilderness of the New World, the Forks of the Ohio appeared to be a most promising opportunity.

His primary mission, though, was not to survey the terrain of the Ohio Country for advantageous strategic positions. Washington had been selected as an unlikely candidate to perform an uncommon duty. The harsh conditions that marked the beginning of Pennsylvania's winter proved to be Washington's first and most immediate difficulty, and staying in one area for too long meant that succumbing to the elements became an all-too-present danger. The unforgiving combination of rain and snow represented a race against time, and time was not a luxury enjoyed by the Virginian. Washington would revisit the Forks of the Ohio again in the future, and during the long trek north he would consider its substantial possibilities countless more times.

The young Washington was a man of great ambition, and he was charged with a monumental task. In accordance with his personal goals and professional duties, he pressed on into the unfamiliar wilderness.

Taming the Wild: European Posturing in the Ohio Country

In an age of colonial supremacy, there was hardly a land so sought after as North America's Ohio Country. Made up of modern-day western Pennsylvania and eastern Ohio, the vast expanse of land captivated European superpowers due to its seemingly endless supply of natural and diplomatic resources. The Ohio Country was an untamed terrain fraught with a wide variety of timber, a prized commodity for European states that, due to extended periods of growth and population, had depleted their own stock. As expansion took place and construction projects boomed, demand for raw materials overseas increased. The heavily wooded forests of North America represented an unimaginable treasure-trove of untapped resources.

The wilds of the Ohio Country were, by today's standards, a lost world. A sweeping wilderness, the landscape was a diverse mixture of heavy forests and broad, flat plains. Inhabited by natives for centuries, the region consisted of thousands of acres that were largely untouched, with resources that were never harvested on a large scale. Trees in these "old growth forests" regularly reached circumferences of more than fifty feet. While there are few examples of these immense trees left in the twenty-first century, the much larger redwoods of America's West Coast offer our best available comparison. The coming of the industrial age, with its high volume of logging and timber removal, erased these natural landmarks from the collective face of the mid-Atlantic region. However, these solemn giants were commonplace in the virgin wilderness of eighteenth-century North America.

Aside from the arboreal benefits made available by the untouched landscape, the Ohio Country also provided some of the continent's most viable populations of diverse and profitable wild game. Large mammals, including deer and elk, permeated the landscape and made hunting an intriguing prospect for settlers still seeking an economic niche to call their own. Along with other large beasts, smaller species used for products other than food, most notably beaver, could be harvested for their highly prized pelts.

These furs were quickly consumed by insatiable European markets. Species of wild birds were plentiful, and ample populations of fish—including species of trout, catfish and salmon—only sweetened the prospects of such an already lucrative territory.

Perhaps the most sought after of all animal byproducts during this period was the pelt of the North American beaver (*Castor canadensis*). Estimated at numbers reaching more than 90 million before Europeans reached the New World, the beavers' pelts soon became high-end commodities and one of North America's most prized resources. Though the animal produced much less usable fur than other native mammals such as the bison, white-tailed deer or elk, it was the unique characteristics of the rodent's hair that made it so valuable. The pelt of the beaver was not like other furs of the period, which were used in a number of different ways but generally for clothing and blankets to supply warmth. In contrast to its fellow mammals, the hair of the beaver possessed tiny barbs that allowed for strong and reliable fabrics to be produced. The minuscule bonds formed between these hairs when woven together created a particularly smooth felt courtesy of their unusual structures.

While not generally desired for large-scale weaving projects, this felt lent itself wonderfully to the specialized craft of hat making. As European gentlemen desired the finest of available headwear, the New World's lucrative fur trade obliged, and the North American beaver quickly became a shrinking commodity.

Navigating the rugged territory of the region was a difficult and taxing ordeal for a number of reasons. Because the area was largely uncharted by Europeans, expeditions into the Ohio Country transformed scouts into explorers and made legends of men. Despite a large number of attempts to accurately define the area, most only experienced small portions, as they had no reliable barometer to accurately measure the full scale of the assignment. Challenges, however, did not end with simply maintaining a constant sense of direction.

To successfully traverse the Ohio Country, one would have relied exclusively on two distinct means of transportation. The first and most widely used were the natural waterways that spider-webbed across the uncharted wilderness. Initially relying on major rivers such as the Allegheny, Beaver and Clarion, scouts would utilize smaller tributaries, such as French Creek in northwestern Pennsylvania, to venture deeper into the woodlands. For the French, who were stationed in colonial outposts in present-day Canada, Lake Erie allowed for a variety of different entry points into the region. The British, however, who trekked from the eastern seaboard, were forced to use river systems exclusively.

The second and more challenging method of navigation was the utilization of footpaths established and maintained by the native groups of the area. Of the most famous of these routes was the Venango Trail, which ran north–south through present-day Allegheny, Butler, Crawford, Venango and Erie Counties. The similarly oriented Catawba Trail touched parts of Greene, Fayette, Westmoreland, Indiana, Jefferson, Elk and McKean Counties. Of the east–west trails, perhaps the most heavily trafficked was the Kittanning Trail that bisected Blair, Cambria, Indiana and Armstrong Counties. The legacy of these footpaths is still seen today, and many of their original routes can still be followed in short legs before disappearing completely.

French Claims

France and Britain were empires at war. With a storied history of conquest between them, the superpowers of Europe found themselves fighting an extended series of small conflicts around the world for territorial dominance. The Americas were just one of many fronts on which these bloody battles were waged, and in time they would be fought as fiercely in the New World as anywhere else on the planet.

Between 1744 and 1748, fighting erupted in what was popularly known as King George's War. While the primary issues remained unresolved at the end of the conflict, both parties became aware that holdings in North America had to be secured and that irrefutable claims had to be made.

For the French, winning the Ohio Country meant consolidating their strategic footholds in North America. With firmly established settlements in Montreal and New Orleans, the American claims of King Louis XV were quite literally a world apart. The key to their continued success and

A casting of the face of an elderly George Washington, rightfully weathered from his many exploits in western Pennsylvania. *Courtesy of the Senator John Heinz History Center.*

stability would be to secure a connection between the two protectorates. In this case, the desired route was a water-bound track beginning in New Orleans and continuing north via the Mississippi River. At the site of Cairo, Illinois, the route would continue northward using the Ohio River until it eventually joined the Allegheny. Acquiring this location, the Forks of the Ohio, was essential to the success of the French imperial initiative in North America. The connection would next snake up the Allegheny until reaching the tributaries of Lake Erie and eventually feed directly into Montreal.

As in any calculated acquisition of property, establishing a foothold in a foreign land required more than tactless displays of military force. In order to win the ultimate prize—in this case, the land and its resources— diplomats were well aware that they first had to win the hearts and minds of the populations that inhabited it. The support of native tribes scattered throughout the Ohio Country was perceived to be the key to domination.

In 1749, colonial officials in Montreal organized an expedition into the Ohio Country to legitimize France's claim to the region. Led by Pierre Joseph

Though British and French plans both included the Forks of the Ohio, the region's Indian populations had coveted the land for decades. Station Square mural. *Courtesy of the author.*

Céleron de Blainville, the diplomatic force met with local tribal representatives in Indian towns throughout the region with the simple petition to consider a partnership with the French Crown. A relationship based on trade, they implored, would benefit their respective tribal affiliations greatly; the only provision would be to deny the British and accept them as a mutual enemy.

The expeditionary force placed six lead plates throughout the region to explicitly claim it for France. A common practice for the time, these markers were installed at the mouths of prominent waterways, including Canwego, French and Wheeling Creeks, as well as the Muskingum River:

> *In the year 1749, of the reign of Louis the 15th, King of France, Céloron, commander of a detachment sent by Monsieur the Marquis de la Galissoniere, Governor General of New France, to reestablish tranquility in some Indian villages of these cantons, have buried this Plate of Lead at the confluence of the Ohio and the Chatauqua, this 29th day of July, near the river Ohio, otherwise Belle Riviere, as a monument of the renewal of the possession we have taken of the said river Ohio and of all those which empty into it, and of all the lands on both sides as far as the sources of the said rivers, as enjoyed or ought to have been enjoyed by the kings of France preceding and as they have there maintained themselves by arms and by treaties, especially those of Ryswick, Utrecht and Aix la Chapelle.*

In their estimation, the French had laid claim to the Ohio Country. The presence of any other imperial interests in the region, most specifically that of the British, would be considered trespassing against the crown of Louis XV. In the spring of 1753, the French declared an act of "communication," and military units descended on the disputed territory to begin the construction of fortifications.

The land now belonged to the French, and they had no intention of leaving it.

British Claims

Though most British colonial holdings were found along the eastern seaboard of North America, there had been encroachments westward beginning in the earliest years of the eighteenth century. To best understand

British claims to the lands of the Ohio Country, though, a brief history of the region's native peoples must first be discussed.

The Iroquois Confederacy was the preeminent Indian sovereignty in the immediate area of the Ohio Country. The Iroquois nation was made up of six unique yet linguistically related tribal units whose territories extended like an arch from western Pennsylvania as far as eastern New York. Known collectively among themselves as the *Hadonasonneh*, or "People of the Longhouse," the Iroquois Confederacy was composed of (from west to east) the Senecas, Cayugas, Onondagas, Oneidas and Mohawks. The sixth tribal unit, the Tuscaroras, was accepted in 1722. Tensions among the Iroquois and other native groups ran historically high, and diplomacy within the New World was just as complex as it was in Europe.

Case in point, the designation of "Iroquois" literally translates into "the Real Adder," a disparaging nickname bestowed on the Six Nations by neighboring tribes in an attempt to gain favor with Europeans.

An artifact of the 1748 Lord Fairfax Line believed to have been left by an expedition of which the teenage Washington was a part. *Courtesy of the Senator John Heinz History Center.*

In the mid-seventeenth century, in an effort to expand their control over the emerging and lucrative fur trade, the Iroquois began a bloody and violent campaign of terror. The goal was to remove potential trade competitors from the Great Lakes region. These conflicts became known collectively as the Beaver Wars. During this operation, the Iroquois successfully vanquished tribal enemies including the Susquehannocks, Eries and Hurons. As a result, the Ohio Country was left virtually abandoned, with the exception of transient Iroquois groups.

Following Queen Anne's War, an international firefight that pitted the British against French, combating parties met in the Dutch city of Utrecht to negotiate peace. The year was 1713. Among the litany of provisions stated in the Treaty of Utrecht was a small addition that stated that the Iroquois would be officially recognized as British subjects. Because the members of the Iroquois Confederacy were officially recognized as British subjects, and because the Iroquois controlled the undefined borders of the Ohio Country following the Beaver Wars, British officials surmised that the Ohio Country was an extension of the British empire.

In what was considered to be an official gesture, the Iroquois and the Colony of Virginia signed the Lancaster Treaty of 1744, giving Britain full rights to the Ohio Country in exchange for a monetary sum of only £400.

The Ohio Company of Virginia

Despite its noble and practical colonial origins, establishing oneself in eighteenth-century America was first and foremost a business venture. While ideals of king and country were brandished proudly on their sleeves, most eager entrepreneurs journeyed to the New World with profit and expansion beating in their hearts. From the beginning of English endeavors in North America, colonial efforts were viewed more as commercial opportunities than as chances to expand imperial borders. In 1606, the now legendary colonists of Jamestown left the British Isles armed with an innovative charter from an investment group known as the Virginia Company of London. With the financial backing of London's most affluent capitalists in tow, exploring the farthest reaches of the earth in search of profit became a feasible reality. It quickly set a groundbreaking precedent.

It was this same modus operandi that gave way to many more land speculation groups across the New World. Although not all were successful, and some were utter failures, the revenue produced by the highest percentile encouraged others to throw their hats into the proverbial ring. Realizing the vast quantities of resources available in the uninhabited Ohio Country, a group of wealthy Virginia colonists combined their collective assets in an attempt to exploit the unclaimed territory for profit. The newly founded Ohio Company of Virginia, as it came to be known, consisted of some of Virginia's most influential social elites. Among those in this group were Colonial Lieutenant Governor Robert Dinwiddie and Thomas Lee, whose direct lineage would include Declaration of Independence signer Richard Henry Lee and Confederate General Robert E. Lee.

Perhaps the most intriguing of the group's distinguished membership, though, was a pair of siblings from eastern Virginia named Lawrence and Augustine Washington. The Washington brothers, like most of their Ohio

The life of the twenty-one-year-old Virginian, George Washington, would change forever in the harsh wilderness of western Pennsylvania.
Courtesy of George Washington's Mount Vernon.

Company associates, earned their wealth and status from the successful cultivation of the tobacco plant. A temperamental and demanding crop, tobacco was, in many ways, the company's primary interest in obtaining land in the Ohio Country. With a cultivation season of nearly fifteen months, tobacco was incredibly challenging to grow but equally profitable and effortless to sell. When the plant grew, it required regular crop rotation, as it drained its host soil of nearly all of its nutritional value. With Virginia's soil becoming increasingly depleted, the Ohio Company saw the unsown soils to the north as a valuable opportunity.

With their collective eyes on the Ohio Country, the Ohio Company funded a local guide named Christopher Gist to establish a base at the northern branch of the Potomac River, at a location known as "Wills Creek." Situated in present-day Cumberland, Maryland, the Wills Creek post would serve as the company's primary entrance point into the uncharted territory to its north.

In 1750, the hardy Gist, carrying the flag of the Ohio Company of Virginia, took the first of many diplomatic missions into the region to engage with local native tribes.

RESPONDING TO THE FRENCH

News of France's exploits in the Ohio Country traveled quickly from the New World to metropolitan London. For the Ohio Company of Virginia, it could not travel fast enough.

In the summer of 1753, France took bold steps to solidify its claims in western Pennsylvania by constructing a series of forts in an attempt to establish a direct line of communication throughout the vaunted wilderness. Oriented from north to south were Forts Presque Isle, Le Boeuf and Machault (a year later in 1754), and though these structures are either considerably refurbished or nonexistent today, their legacy is undeniable. As a result of their initial presence, each fort became a beacon of semicivilization in the heavily forested territory, prompting settlements to develop around them. Today, some of western Pennsylvania's oldest and most historic towns stand in their place. The cities of Erie (Presque Isle), Waterford (Le Boeuf) and Franklin (Machault) can all trace their long heritages back to France's audacious effort to assume control of the Ohio Country.

Ambition

The Ohio Company of Virginia found itself in a unique position in 1753. With extensive French building efforts underway, the shareholders of the company believed that their newly acquired assets were in jeopardy. Unlike other private land speculation groups, however, the Ohio Company had a distinct advantage that gave it special privilege with the British Crown. Lieutenant Governor Robert Dinwiddie, an official subordinate of Parliament *and* a shareholding member of the Ohio Company, enjoyed a direct line of communication with the hub of the British government and used it to his fullest advantage.

By claiming that Britain's, rather than the Ohio Company's, rights were being undermined by its sworn enemies, Dinwiddie set himself apart among colonial officials. Shortly thereafter he was selected as the ideal nominee to organize a mission to remove French influence from the Ohio Country.

Dinwiddie was seen as the provincial leader with the most at stake in this new venture, therefore guaranteeing that it would be carried out with the fullest commitment to success. His mission, as requested by Parliament, was multilayered and quite extraordinary. First and most immediately he was to

The Washington family bible. *Courtesy of the Senator John Heinz History Center.*

demand that the new fortifications built by the French should be vacated at once. Next he was to begin construction of British forts in the region.

After being supplied with munitions to protect these new forts until their completion, most notably cannons and firearms, the venture was underwritten with a strict authorization: use force, if necessary.

DINWIDDIE'S DILEMMA: AN UNLIKELY CHOICE

Robert Dinwiddie was burdened with a tremendous responsibility. Although he had served his king through various means of local government in the American colonies, the decision to confront the French in the wilds of North America had the potential to make him an imperial diplomatic celebrity. Success would carry with it unimaginable opportunities; failure, on the other hand, could prove disastrous for his emerging political career.

His first and most vital decision as organizer would be to select a candidate suited for leading an expedition of this magnitude. The mission needed a man able to see the job completed; more pressing, though, it had to be a man who could represent Great Britain with grace and honor.

Though there was debate as to who would act as the diplomatic face of the mission, there was no question as to who would guide the force. Christopher Gist, who was placed by the Ohio Company at its makeshift base at Wills Creek, had spent the several months exploring the uncharted regions of the Ohio Country. His voyages to the numerous Indian villages of the region produced hopeful results, and he had become a figure that local tribal leaders could trust. He was rugged, durable and, most notably, experienced.

Regardless of who was chosen to lead the diplomatic party, having Gist in tow was an irreplaceable asset to the Ohio Company. It was his presence, and the armed security that came with it, that allowed Dinwiddie to exercise some liberty with his choice of diplomatic leadership.

As a representative of both the Ohio Company of Virginia and the British empire itself, Dinwiddie had a vast pool of resources from which to choose. The game of politics, like the game of business, was one of opportunity. In that same vein, it was also very much a game of *favors*.

More than a year earlier, in June 1752, Lawrence Washington, who had served as chief manager of the Ohio Company, died after an extended bout with tuberculosis at his estate at Mount Vernon. With his death came not only an open position among the leadership of the Ohio Company but also a vacant post as adjutant in the Virginia Militia.

Dinwiddie was selected for the task of assigning the lofty mission due to his equal interests in the empire as well as the Ohio Company, and it would benefit him greatly to enlist the services of a person with ties to both. He recalled a petition received near the time of Lawrence Washington's passing from his younger half-brother, George Washington. George was anxious to replace his older brother in the militia, and Dinwiddie respected his boldness. Recognizing the potential for personal advancement, as well as carrying on his elder brother's legacy, the twenty-year-old George requested that he be assigned the late Lawrence's military position.

Dinwiddie had a fine opinion of the young Washington. He remembered him as a striking figure, standing nearly six feet four inches and carrying a particularly trim frame. As a military man he had little experience to speak of, and his command of the French language was even less impressive. Nevertheless, George Washington was well known among aristocratic social circles, and after spending time surveying in the Blue Ridge Mountains as a teen, he came with the highest of recommendations from William Fairfax. Fairfax was considered royalty in the Virginia colony, and a vote of confidence from him was worth its weight in gold.

George Washington did not hesitate to accept the position after communicating with Dinwiddie and was overjoyed at the assignment. He had dreamed of venturing into the Ohio Country for most of his teen years and relished the opportunity to do so in such a considerable fashion. In 1751, Washington had joined his brother and mentor, Lawrence, on a journey to Barbados. Though he contracted smallpox on the trip, Washington believed himself to be an experienced and savvy explorer. At the age of twenty-one, Washington had a heart bigger than the vast unknown that lay ahead of him, and he was highly confident in his own unproven abilities.

Outwardly, though, Washington was reserved. He made the short journey to Williamsburg to meet with Dinwiddie and discuss the particulars of the mission. Dinwiddie took to the youngster right away and had no regrets about his decision. Washington was composed in their meeting and confidently reassuring. He was a man of common experience but uncommon ambition.

Lieutenant governor
Robert Dinwiddie of
Virginia made the young
Washington an offer he
couldn't refuse. *Courtesy
of the Senator John Heinz
History Center.*

The mission, as explained to Washington, was not over his head. He would first venture north to Wills Creek to join Christopher Gist and other members of their expedition. From there he would continue northward to the Forks of the Ohio and then press on for several days to Fort Le Boeuf. Washington and Gist were to meet with prominent Indian leaders en route and rally support against the French.

On October 31, 1753, Washington left Williamsburg as a man of resolve. He was foolhardy enough to believe that the mission would be easy, but it was also that naiveté that drove him forward.

With a fresh commission—now answering to *Major* George Washington— the young man wrote, "I am sensible my best endeavors will not be wanting."

Chapter 2

CONFIDENCE

Diplomacy in Logstown

JULY 2010

Unlike the city of Pittsburgh, the borough of Ambridge has a firm grasp on its historical identity. Whereas many small towns across America only witness their communities' past in the meager collections of their local historical society, Ambridge has preserved its interpretation of yesteryear in plain sight for all to see. Its contemporary origins reach as far back as 1824, and its residents pay respect to their heritage almost every day.

When passing by the borough alongside the Ohio River, drivers see a large expanse of property seemingly untouched by the corrosive hands of time. The modern world has grown around it, and its antiquated red brick structures reach out to the curious travelers of Route 65. These preserved grounds are the remnants of Old Economy Village, one of the first permanent settlements in the region. From outside the wooden fence that borders the historic site, it is unclear exactly how large the nineteenth-century time capsule really is, but once inside, the relatively small dimensions of the site pale in comparison to its architectural and cultural splendors. Old Economy, as it's known today, stands in nearly perfect condition as a testament to the religious devotions of the millenarian sect that founded it: the Harmonists. History is not hard to find in Ambridge, Pennsylvania, and researchers are more likely to stand next to it than stumble across it in a dense archive.

There is not a clear connection between the modern borough of Ambridge and a settlement of religious isolationists, but like most historic settlements in the Pittsburgh region, there seldom is. Following the gradual decline of the Harmonists at the turn of the century, the property known as Economy was sold to the American Bridge Company in 1905. The acquisition by American Bridge—whose résumé includes San Francisco's Golden Gate Bridge in addition to New York's Brooklyn Bridge—signaled a new age in the history of the area: steel had arrived. Populations in Economy would explode as freshly minted steel mills hungered for laborers and hopeful new immigrants hungered for work. The emerging new town would be renamed for the company responsible for its new lease on life, and it would be forever known as Ambridge.

As seen in most parts of the Pittsburgh region, the arrival of steel greatly changed the way that small boroughs and towns viewed themselves, as well as their past. Ambridge is a textbook example of such a place, for today the town will emphasize its religious and industrial origins, while another chapter of its history serves largely as a footnote. Situated at the intersection of Duss Avenue and Anthony Wayne Drive rests a large stone boulder emblazoned with a plaque. Placed by the Daughters of the Revolution in 1932, the somber reminder reads as follows: "A historic Indian village was located a short distance northwest of this spot…MAJOR GEORGE WASHINGTON held councils at Logstown with Tanacharison, Scarouady, Shingas and other Indian chiefs, November 24 to 30, 1753 while on his important mission to Fort Le Boeuf."

That village was Logstown, a cultural hub of Indian activity and intertribal diplomacy unmatched in the region. To many of those living in Ambridge today, the names listed on the plaque have lost meaning. To most residents, George Washington will bring about a small tinge of patriotic fervor, and to many more the accompanying names will slip away as foreign, alien and inconsequential. Tanacharison…Scarouady…Shingas. Indian names.

Though members of separate tribal units, these were the names of some of the most influential native power brokers in the Ohio Country and key players in the emerging French and Indian War. The role of Native Americans during the conflict between France and England is that they are often portrayed as pawns on a chessboard, tokens in a greater European conflict. However, thanks to the diligent work of historians in the last two decades, a clearer understanding of these enigmatic peoples has developed. This was no game of chess; it was more akin to a high-stakes game of no-limit poker, and the Indians were dealing the cards.

The role of the natives in the Ohio Country may ultimately be remembered as secondary to Washington's in the twenty-first century, but in 1753 the fate of the British empire in North America rested on winning their highly sought favor.

Tanacharison…Scarouady…Shingas. These are names forgotten all too often in modern perspectives, but for young George Washington they were names he would never forget.

November 24, 1753

The mission that George Washington had been given was the opportunity for which he had been waiting since his earliest days of exploration. He was an official representative of the British Crown, and his task was of some consequence. But even more thrilling than the mission itself were the prospective fruits that its successful completion might bear.

The charge was simple enough: deliver a message to the Legardeur de Saint-Pierre, commandant of Fort Le Boeuf. The message was to abandon French claims in the Ohio Country at once, and Washington would deliver it. Although in reality he would serve as nothing more than a representative courier, Washington viewed the approaching meeting as an international summit of the highest order. Dressed in the regal colors typical of an English gentleman, he would stand firm in his presentation and address the French officer with all of the poise and composure of an experienced and confident diplomat.

Presently, though, he was standing exposed in a Pennsylvania winter. His clothes were now heavy with rain and his boots flooded. At the moment, Washington felt anything but dignified.

Aided by Christopher Gist, Washington was confident that he could navigate the untamed wilderness enough to complete his mission and look competent while doing so. After leaving the Forks of the Ohio, the expedition would continue its venture northward courtesy of the icy Ohio River. In the process, a number of smaller matters needed to be addressed, particularly those regarding the region's vast Indian populations. With the right Indian representatives on their side, and likewise on the side of the British, the expedition would most certainly run more smoothly. Gist was an experienced guide and was familiar with the tribal affiliations in the area; more importantly, he was aware of whom specifically they needed to see and where specifically they could be found. His quiet confidence allowed Washington to breathe easy. The good faith of the Ohio Company was bestowed on Washington, but unbeknownst to the young Virginian, he was accompanied by an experienced group of trusted associates that could take command should he at any time falter.

Gist was a recognizable figure to many of the native groups in the Ohio River Valley. A sturdy and reliable man, he displayed a savvy and cunning that had earned him audiences with high-ranking tribal officials in the past. Gist had spent more time in the Ohio Country than most men could ever dream of; he was certainly up to the task of maneuvering an inexperienced young upstart through the dense forests of western Pennsylvania. Alongside Gist was interpreter John Davidson and Barnaby Currin, a fellow Ohio Company employee and former Indian trader. Although they were not the closest of comrades normally, on an outing like this one Currin would serve as Gist's unofficial right-hand man.

Three years earlier, the pair had undertaken a similar expedition farther west into the region of Muskingum, modern-day southeastern Ohio. While encamped at an Indian village on the day after Christmas, the band of Europeans bore witness to the gruesome spectacle of a female prisoner being tortured and killed. In customary fashion, her body was mutilated and left on display by the Indian men of the village—bodies were often mutilated in accordance with the Indian belief that victims would await their killers in the afterlife. If a person was maimed on earth, they would be so in the spirit world as well. As night fell, a group spearheaded by Currin removed the remnants of the young woman from their unholy exhibit and buried her remains. The experienced hardened both men, and though Currin's compassion was a sign of weakness, his resolve impressed Gist greatly.

The first order of business for the fledgling expedition was to meet with, and fall into the good graces of, the Iroquois Confederacy. Scaling a large swath of territory extending from eastern New York to eastern Ohio, the Iroquois Confederacy was the preeminent Indian power in the Ohio

Country. To better facilitate operations and maintain control, the Iroquois developed a system of regional representation in the form of assigned "Half-Kings." As the highest-ranking Iroquois in his proposed sphere of influence, the Half-King would speak on behalf of the Six Nations and meet with any prominent diplomats passing through his area. Because of its sheer size, the Ohio Country had many Half-Kings, and Gist's firsthand information regarding the local representative made an audience with him essential to the success of the mission.

The Half-King they sought was named Tanacharison. An imposing figure, Tanacharison relocated to the Ohio Country in 1748 to claim his position and was well respected by the various Indian groups he represented. His reign as Half-King was exceptional, and his influence was sure to be a valuable asset. As a diplomat, the native Seneca had met personally with French explorer Céleron de Blainville in 1749, as well as British Indian agent George Croghan, just a few months before Washington's expedition. In his youth, Tanacharison saw his father struck down and slain by French settlers, and despite his resulting prejudices, he remained a gracious and cordial ambassador. Gist was well aware, though, that an opportunity to oppose the French was one that Tanacharison was unlikely to refuse.

The Half-King held court at the Indian village of Logstown, site of modern-day Ambridge, Pennsylvania. Composed of many different native groups, including Iroquois, Shawnee, Delawares and Mohicans, Logstown had become a busy center of activity and a vital stop for any diplomatic party traveling on the Ohio River. Originally settled by the Shawnee as early as 1725, the site was further improved by the French in 1748 as a means of enticing its native inhabitants.

In order to enter Logstown safely and receive an audience with the Half-King, the party of Europeans would require a high-ranking Indian representative to join them. Washington himself was terribly inexperienced when it came to dealing directly with Indians, and the stories of their ceremonial eccentricities made him hesitant to declare any orders without first consulting his fellow team members. Gist recommended that they first meet with Shingas, a Delaware representative with heavy political sway in Logstown.

Two miles north of the forks, the canoes crawled slowly up the Ohio River until the fires of settlement could be seen. It was midafternoon, and

Washington at the Point, artist John Buxton's incredible pictorial account of George Washington standing at the Forks of the Ohio, awaiting his meeting with the Half-King. *Courtesy of John Buxton.*

Washington was preparing for his first official duties as a British diplomat. The journey from shore to camp was a steep climb up the muddy banks of the river, and Washington once again found himself in a less-than-graceful situation. The camp was cold, the sky was dismal and it lacked the certain elements of exotic danger that Washington had come to expect. Originally scouted by Ohio Company officials as the site for a possible encampment, the camp of the Delaware king was small, although its position did have strategic value.

The exact position of Shingas' camp is unknown, but from clues left in Washington's journal it can be placed, with some uncertainty, along the Ohio River between present-day McKees Rocks, Pennsylvania, and Bellevue, Pennsylvania: "About two miles from this, on the southeast side of the river, at the place where the Ohio Company intended to erect a fort, lives Shingiss, king of the Delawares. We called upon him, to invite him to council at the Logstown."

Gist led the party to Shingas' cabin, a commanding force of habit that was not troubling to the young major at that moment. The structure in which the Delaware resided was not unlike the others in camp and was quite typical for the period. With Gist greeting his old friend, Washington would have noted the smokiness of the space from the small fire burning for warmth, as well as the firearms that Shingas would have acquired from the many trading connections of Logstown itself. Discussing the urgency of the situation, Gist convinced Shingas to take his team upriver to the village that same evening, and after some much-needed (yet brief) respite, the expedition pressed on.

For Washington, his first diplomatic experience in an Indian village was uneventful, but his meeting at Logstown would be anything but disappointing.

Nightfall in Logstown

The trek from Shingas' Delaware village to Logstown was a taxing one. Although the expedition had moved with little problem from Virginia to Maryland and farther to the Forks of the Ohio, the weather was becoming more than a nuisance to Washington, Gist and their men. The current of the Ohio River had been helpful to Washington until this point, but Shingas and his Indian aid Lawmolach insisted that, with weather changing as it had been, the best alternative would be to reach Logstown on foot. The expedition's horses would bear the burden.

The outing itself was not difficult, certainly not as difficult as the journey ahead, but Washington's personal writings do give some indication of the hardships: "We traveled over some extremely good and bad land to get to this place." The terrain that separates modern Pittsburgh, the suggested origin, and Ambridge, Pennsylvania, is uniform in its diverse orientation. Consisting of a series of peaks and valleys running parallel to the river, one can gain a sense of its makeup by driving northbound on Route 65, passing the boroughs of Avalon, Emsworth and Sewickley. Although the road itself is flat due to its proximity to the river, glances to the north will reveal the topographical features that Washington described as "bad land."

As the expeditionary force closed in on Logstown, the sun was setting in front of them. The sky was rich with deep hues of violet and red, and the sounds of settlement could be heard in the distance. For Washington, his first glimpses of the village itself were not what he would have expected considering Shingas' village. Remodeled by the French in 1748, Logstown now consisted of many European-style log cabins. Though these cabins were surrounded by more traditional Iroquoian-style longhouses, it was clear that he was entering a community in the midst of change.

Gist had explained to Washington the significance of the Half-King before their arrival to the village, and the significance of the meeting was not lost on the major. As they moved about the streets, Washington remained stone-faced, while his mind fluttered at the sounds of alien tongues all around him. Peddlers of animal furs and firearms could be heard hawking their goods, and the convergence of native cultures enlightened him to the true diversity of the region's Indian populace. Gist and Washington were careful not to press Shingas too abruptly for an immediate audience with the Half-King, but they did alert him to their urgency.

The team meandered excitedly through Logstown, well aware of the apparent haste under which it had been constructed. Unlike the colonial settlements that Washington had been raised in, there was nothing permanent about the Indian village. The most stable structures in Logstown were the cabins built by the French five years earlier, and even they were of questionable condition. It was almost as though, Washington thought, the entire village could be abandoned at a moment's notice.

Suddenly the major was snapped backed to reality by the news that was received by Shingas and relayed by their interpreter John Davidson: the Half-King was not in the village.

The expedition members were disappointed, but they were assured that he would return by morning. In the meantime, Davidson explained, they would be able to sit and engage with the remaining native representatives still in the village. Washington understood the importance of this congress, despite the fact that Tanacharison himself would not be present. Though they did not carry the esteem of the Half-King, these were powerful men nonetheless.

The meeting was held in one of the large French cabins of the village. Participating in lieu of Tanacharison was the Iroquoian representative known to the Shawnee in the village as Monacatootha, although his given name was Scaroyada, "side of the sky." He was accompanied by a small number of other sachems, or chiefs, for which there is little evidence of names. Washington, with Gist and Davidson for support, greeted Scaroyada with a traditional series of ceremonial gifts. Upon greeting the sachem, the young Virginian presented a wampum belt, followed by a twist of Virginia

*An Indian War Chief Completely
Equipped with Scalp in Hand,*
George Townshend, 1751–58.
*Courtesy of the Senator John Heinz
History Center.*

tobacco. While the tobacco was a gift of a more practical nature, the wampum belt held a special significance to the Indians of the Ohio Country. Made traditionally of colored shells and measuring up to six feet in length, the presentation of the wampum belt was an official announcement that diplomatic proceedings were to begin.

With all the grace and steadfastness that Washington had hoped to portray, he spoke to the subordinates of the Half-King and eloquently presented his duties as a British official. Scaroyada understood their desire to see Tanacharison in person and explained to the group, through the interpreter Davidson, that the Half-King "was at his hunting cabin on Little Beaver creek about fifteen miles off." Washington wrote further that he "desired him to send for the half king, which he promised to do by a runner in the morning, and for other sachems."

The already present chiefs were impressed by his poise and were happy to furnish a meeting when prompted.

MEETING THE HALF-KING

After the gathering, Washington and his team were escorted to their sleeping quarters for the night. To ensure that the meeting would end on a civil (and, more importantly, *even*) note, Washington and Gist invited the tribal representatives back to their assigned resting places. Though the earlier discussions had gone well, Washington and Gist were both aware that an invitation for further pleasantries would not leave the Virginians obliged to their hosts in any way. This, in theory, would allow for a meeting with the Half-King to be held under level conditions.

The morning of November 25 was a clear one. When Washington awoke, rested and grateful for a more comfortable night's rest than he was growing used to, there was excitement among the villagers of Logstown. Expecting the Half-King's presence, the young major rushed to make himself presentable, but not in such a way as to appear overly excited in front of Gist and the others. Upon leaving his tent, Washington was surprised to see not Tanacharison but rather four French soldiers.

Though it was not the scene he anticipated, it was an opportunity nevertheless. Washington approached the men and introduced himself accordingly. As military men, they certainly would have responded to Washington's recently acquired title of major, though they all had significantly more military experience than Washington himself.

Following a long inquisition, Washington learned a great deal about both the men and the state of the French military in North America. The soldiers explained that they were recent deserters originally stationed in New Orleans. Assigned to transfer one hundred men and eight canoes worth of supplies to the French forts situated south of Lake Erie, they explained that their recent journey took them up the Mississippi River to the point where the large waterway joined with the Ohio River (modern-day Cairo, Illinois). The four weary infantrymen continued by explaining that they were scheduled to meet a group similar to their own at Kuskuskas; the group never arrived. It was at that point that they deserted their colors and fled south to Shannoah Town (Portsmouth, Ohio) and proceeded to Logstown. Their ultimate goal was to reach the British city of Philadelphia.

Neither Washington nor Gist wrote further about the men's motivations for abandoning their posts, but the lucrative business that trade had become for private citizens within the limits of the Ohio Country should have been

As depicted in this eighteenth-century image, children were frequently kidnapped during raids and, though sometimes killed, were often absorbed into the tribal fabric of Indian life. *Courtesy of the Senator John Heinz History Center.*

reason enough. Experienced military men would have had all of the physical and mental tools needed for success. Like their intentions, it remained to be seen why their awaited French comrades never arrived. There is some light to be shed on their story, however. The scheduled meeting point called Kuskuskas was actually quite well known in the region and is now the site of New Castle, Pennsylvania. As a former Delaware village, Kuskuskas was an instrumental meeting point in local Indian politics.

Back in his quarters, Washington took careful notes of their discussion in his journal and relished in the quiet that allowed him to write so clearly. Commotion, however, soon startled him for the second time that day, and Washington was well aware of the nature of this new excitement: the Half-King had finally arrived.

The young Virginian hurriedly placed his journal back within the confines of his supplies for safekeeping. Seeking out his interpreter Davidson, Washington planned on approaching Tanacharison immediately. As they rounded the corner of the cabin, the major and his translator took careful note of the sight ahead of them. Accompanied by an informal delegation of men, each carrying their own respective firearms and meager trophies of small game, was the Half-King.

An older man, Tanacharison was of average height but moved with a considerable air of respect. With traditional tattoos on his face, chest and arms, the outward appearance of strength displayed by the Half-King struck Washington. Time was not on the Half-King's side, however, as lines of aging creased his face and visible scars accentuated his hands. While the exact birth date of Tanacharison is not known, his death is well documented. He died of pneumonia in October 1754, less than one year after his first meeting with Washington.

When Washington was finally able to address Tanacharison, there was once again surprisingly little initial pomp and circumstance surrounding the conversation. The Half-King knew of the British force's arrival and, though solicited rather abruptly, was welcoming. Through translation, Washington greeted the Seneca and thanked him for his short-notice return. After some pleasantries, Washington extended an invitation back to his tent to discuss more pertinent and pressing issues.

The Half-King accepted.

OPENING REMARKS: A COUNTRY BETWEEN

The Virginians had been in Logstown for a full day, and the Half-King was preparing to join them shortly. Though Tanacharison had a larger home that was certainly more suitable for a meeting than the meager tent of Washington, the Iroquoian diplomat had been officially invited, and he was required to attend. He was acting as an emissary of the Iroquois Confederacy, the Six Nations, the *Hadonnesoneh*—his personal reservations had to be dismissed. Likewise, as a representative in his own right, Washington would need to *extend* an invitation rather than *accept* one. His actions, too, were a reflection of the British empire. For Washington, the meeting would be a milestone in his professional career. Unlike his initial meeting with the Delaware Shingas a day earlier, Washington would host the Half-King without the subtle supervision of Christopher Gist. Joined only by his interpreter Davidson, the twenty-one-year-old would attempt to broker an alliance between the British empire and one of the most powerful Indian leaders in the Ohio Country. Unwavering composure would be essential, and even the slightest of ambassadorial follies could cause irreparable damage.

The men studied each other as they commenced their discussions, both exchanging pleasantries while awaiting the subject of French imperial ambitions to turn the tide of the dialogue. It would be the Virginian who would first initiate the deliberation, as he was the visiting party. The discussions of the expeditions' ultimate intentions granted the Half-King the opportunity to mention his most recent diplomatic experience with the French, now fortified in the Ohio Country. In September, just two months before, Tanacharison had participated in council at Presque Isle, France's northernmost fortification in the Ohio Country. In attendance there was a French officer who introduced himself as Pierre Paul Sieur de Marin. Washington listened to the Half-King intently and made mental notes of the procedures surrounding the description of the wilderness mediation with the French.

The curiosity of Washington was endearing to Tanacharison, and his youthful approach to his assignment created a palpable atmosphere of excitement in their discussions. The Half-King claimed that the proceedings were regarded in "a very stern manner" by the French and that his treatment was "abrupt." Washington wrote of Tanacharison's account of the events and relays the speech that he delivered verbatim:

> *Fathers, I am come to tell you your own speeches; what your own mouths have declared. Fathers, You, in former Days, set a Silver Basin before us, wherein there was the leg of a beaver, and desired of all Nations to come and eat of it; to eat in peace and plenty, and not to be churlish to one another; and that if any such person should be found to be a disturber, I*

here lay down by the Edge of the dish a rod, which you must scourge them with; and if I your Father, should get foolish, in my old days, I desire you may use it upon me as well as others.

Now Fathers, it is you that are the disturbers in this land, by coming and building your towns, and taking it away unknown to us, and by Force…

Fathers, I desire you may hear me in civilness; if not, we must handle that rod which was laid down for the use of the obstreperous. If you had come in a peaceable manner, like our brothers the English, we should not have been against your trading with us, as they do; but to come, fathers, and build great houses upon our land, and to take it by force, is what we cannot submit to.

Fathers, both you and the English are white, we live in a country between; therefore the land belongs to neither one nor to other; But the Great Being Above allowed it to be a place of residence for us; so Fathers, I desire you to withdraw, as I have done our Brothers the English; for I will keep you at arms length. I lay this down as a trial for both, to see which will have the greatest Regard to it, and that Side we will stand by, and make equal Sharers with us.

Our Brothers the English have heard this, and I come now to tell it to you, for I am not afraid to discharge you off this Land.

Washington also noted Tanacharison account of Marin's response:

Now, my Child, I have heard your speech, you spoke first, but it is my time to speak now. Where is my wampum that you took away, with the marks of towns in it? This Wampum I do not know, which you have discharged me off the Land with; but you need not put yourself to the Trouble of Speaking, for I will not hear you; I am not afraid of flies, or mosquitoes, for Indians are such as those; I tell you, down that river I will go, and will build upon it, according to my command; if the River was backed up, I have forces sufficient to burst it open, and tread under my feet all that stand in opposition, together with their alliances; for my force is as the sand upon the sea shore; Therefore, here is your Wampum, I fling it at you. Child, you talk foolish; you say this Land belongs to you, but there is not the back of my nail yours; I saw that land sooner than you did, before the Shannoahs and you were at War; lead was the man that went down, and took possession of that River; it is my land, and I will have it, let who will stand up for, or say against it. I'll buy and sell with the Englaish (mocking). If people will be ruled by me, they may expect kindness, but not else.

As the long evening of conversation came to a close, both Tanacharison and Washington agreed to continue their accord the following day, each with much more to discuss. The young Virginian next escorted the Half-King from his tent, located his journal and began to transcribe the events that had just transpired.

THE PROPOSAL

As the sun settled on the horizon and evening fell on November 26 (at a time identified by Washington as nine o'clock), the parties met once again, this time at the longhouse of Tanacharison. Joining them now was Christopher Gist, as well as Scaroyada and more tribal representatives from across the region. With a larger, potentially more influential, council in session, Washington began his appeal. With two full days of duty now under his proverbial belt in Logstown, he beamed with confidence:

Brothers, I have called you together in Council, by Order of your Brother the Governor of Virginia, to acquaint you that I am sent, with all possible Dispatch, to visit, and deliver a Letter to the French Commandant, of very great Importance to your Brothers the English; and I dare say, to you their Friends and Allies.

I was destined, brothers, by your brother, the governor, to call upon you, the sachems of the nations, to inform you of it, and to ask your advice and assistance to proceed the nearest and best road to the French, You see, brothers, I have gotten this far on my Journey.

His Honor likewise desired me to apply to you for some of your young men to conduct and provide provisions for us on our way, and be a safeguard against those French Indians who have taken up the hatchet against us. I have spoken thus particularly to you, brothers, because his Honor, our governor, treats you as good friends and allies, and holds you in great esteem. To confirm what I have said, I give you this string of wampum.

Whereas the speech recounted by Washington in his journal was executed with accuracy and precision, the reality of the situation was such that few, if any, of the sachems present were able to comprehend his message to any meaningful extent. John Davidson would have stood alongside the major to transmit his message in Tanacharison's native Iroquoian language. The result was a clamor of foreign tongues debating Washington's message. With Tanacharison considering all of the opinions of his fellow natives, he rose and spoke:

> *I rely upon you as a brother ought to do, as you say we are brothers and one people. We shall put heart in hand and speak to our fathers, the French, concerning the speech they made to me, and you may depend that we will endeavor to be your guard.*
>
> *Brother, as you have asked my advice, I hope you will be ruled by it, and stay until I can provide a company to go with you. The French speech-belt is not here; I have to go for it to my Hunting-Cabin. Likewise, the people whom I have ordered in are not yet come, and cannot until the third night from this; until which time, brother, I must beg you to stay.*
>
> *I intend to send a Guard of Mingo, Shannoahs, and Delaware, that our brothers may see the love and loyalty we bear them.*

The Half-King's response was not what Washington had hoped it would be. Unwilling to present a definite response to the Virginian's proposition, Tanacharison declared that further council with Delawares and Shannoahs would be necessary. In an attempt at diplomatic posturing, Washington quickly rose to his feet:

> *I thanked him in the most suitable manner I could; and told him that my business required the greatest expedition, and would not admit of that delay. He was not well pleased that I should offer to go before the time he had appointed, and told me that he could not consent to our going without a guard, for Fear some Accident should befall us, and draw a reflection upon him; besides, says he, this is a Matter of no small moment, and must not be entered into without due consideration.*

At stake was a pan-Indian force to join in alliance with the British empire, a maneuver that could forever change the face, and fate, of the Ohio Country.

Chapter 3

VERSATILITY

Setting Out

NOVEMBER 26, 1753

Washington had returned to his tent shortly after offering his proposal to the Half-King and the sachems. Though he had delivered it well, he did not receive a response in a manner as quickly as he would have liked; he was aware that decisions like this one were rarely made in haste. Washington and Gist discussed the council, and the latter viewed it favorably, but his positive outlook did little to console the young major. In truth, it really was not intended to.

NOVEMBER 27, 1753

Washington awoke the next morning to find the Half-King conspicuously absent and, upon further investigation, discovered that he was true to his word. Before dawn Tanacharison had ordered a party of runners to appeal to the chiefs and sachems of the Shannoahs. The Half-King himself was on a separate journey to his Beaver Creek hunting cabin to obtain a belt of wampum in preparation for any French representatives he might receive.

The Virginia expedition was well aware that any further actions would be ill advised without the Half-King present, so the members took advantage

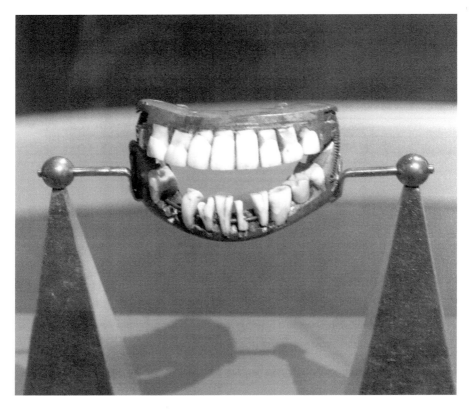

Though they weren't wooden as legend suggests, Washington's infamous false teeth were largely composed of animal bone. *Courtesy of the Senator John Heinz History Center.*

of the brief respite to resupply their packs and rest their weary bodies after two weeks of near constant trekking since leaving Williamsburg. At midday, Washington was running any number of possible scenarios through his mind and, for the first time in many days, was *not* writing in his journal. Gist and the others were reviewing their stock of more practical necessities and discussing possible routes of travel with some of the more empathetic natives in Logstown. While most of the Virginians were beginning to pack and were occupied by smaller errands, a familiar Indian figure approached. It was Scaroyada.

Joining the chief of the Iroquois was a new face unfamiliar to Washington. Gist recognized him and claimed that his name was Pollatha Wapia. Not much is known of Pollatha Wapia today, but his actions lead historians to believe that his political position was akin to the Half-King's. The Indian delegation brought with them a number of supplies, some more sensible than others. The act was a gesture of goodwill that was much appreciated by the Virginians.

NOVEMBER 28, 1753: "MASTERS OF THE OHIO"

Washington and the Virginians had certainly enjoyed their day of rest, but every member of the expedition was aware that the worst of the Pennsylvania winter was ahead of them. The Half-King had not yet returned, and the runners sent to the Shannoahs were still nowhere in sight. Time was running out and Washington was growing restless.

The men slept comfortably through the night, but as the next day crept slowly into the next evening, their patience was wearing thin. They did not know, however, that their wait would not be much longer. As dusk began to settle, Tanacharison returned to camp, and the Virginians were expecting him shortly. A member of his party informed Washington and Gist that the Half-King requested to address them; the Virginians offered their tent for the council.

Tanacharison appeared in the tent not long after. Joining him was his primary advocate, Scaroyada, as well as two other influential sachems. Washington was becoming more familiar with Indian customs and was growing quite fond of the added attention he was receiving as a British diplomat. Tanacharison did not quibble with the Virginians, as he had done in the past, because the purpose of the council was to simply pass on some news received from the Venango region.

As proceedings began, it was Scaroyada, not the Half-King, who took the floor. The message that he transferred was one of a particular interest to the Virginians as representatives of the British empire. The story that the Iroquois relayed described a meeting called by the French involving many important Indian tribes, including, most prominently, the Delawares (or Lenni-Lenape). The French informed the gathering of Indian peoples that "they intended to have been down river this fall, but the waters were growing cold, and the winter advancing, which obliged them to go into quarters." The French had not yet established a firm, fortified position as far south as

Images like this one of Washington during the American Revolution pervade the modern consciousness, but history shows that the Virginian was not always so gallant. *Courtesy of George Washington's Mount Vernon.*

the Forks of the Ohio, but their announcement made it clear that they would arrive to do so during the spring thaw.

The meeting was not simply a declaration, nor a proposition, but rather a warning. The French desired that the Indians of the region "might be quite passive, and [should] not intermeddle unless they had a mind to draw all their force upon them."

Upon further inquisition by the Virginians, it was revealed that this warning was delivered by French Indian agent and interpreter Phillipe-Thomas Chabert de Joncaire, a Montreal native known to the Indians as "Nitachinon"; Scaroyada continued his story. The French "expected to fight the English three Years…in which Time they should conquer, but if they should prove equally strong, that they and the English would join to cut them all off, and divide the land between them."

The Frenchman Joncaire delivered one final caveat to those tribal representatives in council: though they had lost "some few of their

The figure of the Seneca Tanacharison plays heavily on Washington's experiences in the Pittsburgh region. *Courtesy of the Senator John Heinz History Center.*

Soldiers...there were Men enough to reinforce them, and make them Masters of the Ohio."

The French had made their position clear. The Indians of the Ohio River Valley were now aware that soldiers would arrive by spring. Whether their arrival was peaceful or aggressive would be a matter of how willing the native peoples were to stay out of their way.

NOVEMBER 29, 1753: THE DECISION TO REMAIN

Another day passed in Logstown, and Washington, along with his men, was losing faith in the Half-King's pledge. The true heart of the mission was the delivery of a verbal warning to the French fortified within the Ohio Country, not to secure Indian allegiances. If word returned to Lieutenant Governor Dinwiddie that progress had slowed to such a pace, Washington feared that he, too, would be regarded as ineffective. While he was not discrediting his native hosts completely, the twenty-one-year-old's nerves were rattled to say the least.

Tanacharison was not blind to the concerns of his guests, and he and Scaroyada made Washington and his men their top priority. Early on November 29, the Half-King and his consul made an unexpected appearance at the tents of the Virginians. Their intentions were those of anxious men.

The Half-King implored the Virginians to remain for one day longer and made known his understanding of the expedition's concerns. Washington listened intently as Tanacharison explained that the Shannoahs possessed a string of wampum of vast importance and that any action taken against the French would be impossible without it. This wampum, the Half-King continued, was the equivalent of a European treaty, a physical manifestation of an official alliance between the Shannoahs and the French. Without it in hand, any gesture would be seen as wholly unsanctioned and therefore invalid.

Washington wrote, "When I found them so pressing in their request, and knew that returning of wampum was the abolishing of agreements; and giving this up, was shaking off all dependence upon the French, I consented to stay, as I believe an offence offered at this crisis, might be attended with greater ill consequence, Than another Day's Delay."

The intricacies of Indian diplomacy remained foreign to Washington, but the commitment to maintaining their principles impressed him. He would do everything in his power to see that these agreements were fundamentally strong and of unquestionable authenticity; if that meant remaining at Logstown until the wampum arrived, he would do so. The Half-King continued by explaining that aside from the allegiance of the Shannoahs, there were other matters that required more time—particularly that of the Delawares. As a Delaware sachem, the presence of Shingas would be instrumental in maintaining his tribe's commitment, but it was not as vital as acquiring the Delaware string of wampum. It, too, was not in Logstown.

Versatility

Tanacharison explained that Shingas would be unable to attend to the Virginians and, more importantly, the British in person because his wife had fallen ill. On a positive note, the Half-King added, the Delaware wampum was securely in the hands of a reliable ally. Known as Custaloga, the person in question was also a Delaware sachem who could be found in Venango, though he normally inhabited the region of French Creek in northern Pennsylvania. The men agreed that a council would need to be made as the expedition trekked north to acquire this precious asset. Just before exiting, the Indian delegation conceded that if the Shannoah wampum did not arrive by evening, Washington and his men were free to press on. Tanacharison and Scaroyada expressed their gratitude and commitment, as well as a guarantee that they would send runners to deliver the belated wampum if delayed any longer; they then left the Virginians to their duties.

Washington was becoming overwhelmed by the density of the task at hand and wondered if his administrators in Virginia had any understanding of the complexity of Indian diplomacy. Any preconceived European notions of these peoples were certainly dispelled in his mind, and he was grateful to have such a capable and experienced team around him. Without the efforts of Christopher Gist, John Davidson and Barnaby Currin, he would have been lost in the tangled web of antiquated rituals. Washington commenced the arduous task of updating his journal in anticipation of the Shannaohs' arrival as the day wore on.

The chilling winds of the emerging winter whistled through Washington's tent, and he was thankful for the meager shelter that he was given. He pitied those outside in the weather and nearly forgave the Shannoahs for their tardiness—that is, until he realized that in a day's time he, too, would be hiking through those same unforgiving elements. Darkness had overtaken the landscape, and there was still no sign of the expected Indian envoy. Washington and Gist agreed that they would begin to head north at day break. Just as the men were settling in for the night, the Half-King appeared outside of their makeshift camp. The news was not promising.

The Shannoahs had not yet arrived, explained Tanacharison, and Washington would not be leaving with their wampum in tow. However, with great promise in his voice, Tanacharison explained the Iroquois commitments in some detail. As a native Seneca, and therefore a member of the Six Nation Iroquois Confederacy, the Half-King's assistance was vastly more important than any that could be provided by the smaller tribes of the region. He continued by reciting a speech to the Virginians declaring any existing alliances the French as extinguished and explained that it would be repeated verbatim across the Six Nations by his fellow sachem Jeskakake. Jeskakake, an elderly yet regal man, was himself a Cayuga chief, and his delivery of such a speech would resonate greatly to show the full allegiance of the Iroquois people.

Recent communications with Shingas had also brought good news. Although he would still be unable to attend because of his wife's declining condition, he did deliver a string of wampum to be given to Custaloga at Venango. While wampum was used to confirm a treaty between two separate parties, it could also be used a mechanism of delivering orders from one representative to another. This wampum would be understood by Custaloga to mean only one thing: deliver his wampum to the French and end their alliance. With this, the Half-King became quite serious, so much so that Washington was unable to remove his gaze from the powerful Seneca.

From his pack, the Half-King removed a string of wampum unlike one that Washington had ever seen before. That designation was not so impressive, considering that Washington had seen very few, but the severity of Tanacharison's expression indicated that this was no ordinary string of shells. It was black and white, rather mundane in comparison to some of the more elaborate and colorful examples he had seen before. Bold in its simplicity, Tanacharison explained that this was the wampum of the Iroquois Confederacy—it was a final warning. The message that Jeskakake was to deliver was a warning not unlike the one that Washington himself was meant to express: the French were to abandon their posts and leave the Ohio Country.

The Iroquois wampum, though, was not intended for the French. Should the French refuse their request (which they most certainly would), the black-and-white string was to be delivered immediately and directly to the Six Nations in Upstate New York. It would signify the refusal of not just *a* warning but rather of a *third* and *final* warning. The Indians of the Ohio Country traditionally granted an enemy three warnings before officially declaring war against them. The first of these warnings had been delivered by the council of natives at Venango during the meeting held by Captain Joncaire and the second by Tanacharison himself at his meeting with Pierre Paul Sieur de Marin just two months earlier (see the second chapter).

The Half-King completed his strategic explanation to the Virginians and then declared that he must depart to the council house of Logstown to discuss matters further. The topic of conversation would be how many men the Half-King and his fellow chiefs would choose to send with the Virginians on their journey. For those in the expedition, it was the most critical issue discussed during their entire stay in Logstown.

Neither Washington nor his men were invited.

November 30, 1753: Brothers in Arms

Washington and Gist debated the potential outcome of the Logstown council throughout the night and early morning. The major respected the situation of the sachems for requesting privacy as they deliberated among themselves, but now, more comfortable in his position of diplomat, he felt slighted by his exclusion. Considering the generally positive outcomes of the proceedings to this point, Washington felt comfortable in assuming that a large envoy of natives would be accompanying his small expedition as their ventured north; Gist, though, was not so confident.

Just days earlier, Washington argued, the Half-King spoke of an extensive force that would transform the current Virginian force into a formidable division. After witnessing the devotion of Tanacharison, the young major refused to accept that anything less would be produced. Gist, however, disagreed. Always the pragmatist (a necessary attribute on a journey such as this), Gist claimed that a force as large as Washington expected would be unnecessary and only serve to draw attention to their movements. He had expected much less.

The evening did not yield the answers that Washington and Gist so anxiously awaited, and they had to wait until morning to receive any definitive word. The young major prepared for a night's rest while peering inquisitively toward the village's large common council house. He could not see the chiefs inside, but the subdued fires that blazed within made the seams between its timber walls flicker with a mysterious orange tint.

It was at that moment that Washington finally understood the paradoxical fascination that Europeans had with the native peoples of the Americas. They existed like a counterculture in a land that time had seemingly forgotten. They were the antithesis of the ideals that eighteenth-century Europe so proudly exemplified. There was a formal savagery in the way that they did business; their daily rituals were so mundane and archaic that most would see them as futile. It was then that he knew that any decision made would be final and that it would be made in the best interest of their collective tribes. Washington could only hope that it would be in the best interests of Britain as well.

In the morning, Washington's long-awaited result was delivered in prompt fashion. The Virginians knew that regardless of the sachems' decision the expedition would be moving north that day; their demeanors were cold, hardy and focused. Washington and Gist met with the Half-King in the open streets of Logstown along with their entire party. They were ready to move, and the outward appearance of determination to continue was instrumental to their cause.

Tanacharison awaited the major in the open, chilly air and greeted him with a stern gaze; he was also determined. Washington approached the Half-King with Gist and, remaining respectful, abruptly inquired about the sachems' verdict. The Seneca wasted no time: it had been decided that three chiefs and one hunter would be joining the expedition.

Washington felt his heart sink at the news. He had not acquired the large Indian force as per Dinwiddie's instructions. He saw his first task slip away, a failure. Gist was quite pleased with the decision, however, and Washington, after observing his guide's reaction, grew more open to the contribution. The Half-King explained that "a greater number might give the French suspicion of some bad design, and cause them to be treated rudely." Washington was instantly suspicious. After two days waiting for a party of Shannoahs that never arrived, as well as a wampum that was never recovered, he believed he had the right to be doubtful. "I rather think that they could not get their hunters in," he later wrote.

The Half-King now introduced those who would be joining them. The numbers of the party had been decided by the sachems the previous night at the council house, but the actual candidates selected fell on the feet of Tanacharison. They would all be capable, they would all be experienced and, most notably, they would all be Iroquois.

The first of the three chiefs announced was Jeskakake. This decision was of no surprise to the Virginians, as Tanacharison had previously mentioned that it would be Jeskakake who would deliver the ultimatum to the French commandant at Venango. Gist and Washington paid their respects to the sachem as the Half-King continued. The next introduced was a Seneca like Tanacharison. He was called White Thunder but was also known throughout the Ohio Country as "Kaghswaghtaniunt." It was his third alias that was most comforting to Washington, though, as he was also called "Belt of Wampum." Clearly experienced, White Thunder would be a welcomed addition to the convoy.

Announced next was "the Hunter." A young man, noticeably older than Washington himself but more powerful in his build, the Hunter would serve as the physical arm of the sachems. He, too, was a Seneca and was held in high esteem within Logstown. Strong, brave and only thirty-three years of age, he was expected to be a valuable asset to the expedition. His name was Guyasuta.

Coarse in comparison to the older members of his delegation, the demeanor of the Hunter expressed his true opinion of the mission. He

French Creek, 1753: Half-King and Christopher Gist, artist John Buxton's work showing Tanacharison and Gist contemplating their next move in the wilderness. *Courtesy of John Buxton.*

was not acting on behalf of the British or for the greater benefit of any European power; he was a servant of the Indians of the Ohio Country. In his gaze alone, Guyasuta made it clear that he was not particularly fond of Washington or his men.

With three-quarters of their new party now assembled, Washington silently awaited the next nomination. Tanacharison stood stone-faced in front of them, and the perplexed major shot a confused glance at Christopher Gist. A sly smile appeared on the guide's face, and Washington was now more puzzled than before.

It was only after a second glance toward his Indian hosts that the young Virginian realized the significance of the contribution before them: the fourth member of their new expedition would be the Half-King himself.

Moving as One

With their new alliance still freshly minted, the team prepared for the hike. It was a scene of subdued celebration as Washington, along with Gist, his team and their new Indian comrades marched through the makeshift streets of Logstown. The Half-King garnered respect and recognition wherever he went, and the only farewells that the group received were directed at the Seneca and his fellow sachems. Washington likely reflected on the realization that they probably would not be missed at all if not for their new association with Tanacharison. It was nine o'clock in the morning.

The group set out on the long-established and well-traveled route northward toward Venango. As they had done in their times together before arriving at Logstown, the Virginians maintained very little conversation, as their energies were placed solely on the monotonous march ahead of them—one hoof in front of the other and miles to go. Though he was tolerant of the ramble, Washington had never been one for long-distance riding. As a boy he had spent a large amount of time riding his family's horses in the wilderness of Virginia, but never at any length such as this. He considered the strenuous hike as part of the journey, a small consequence of such a magnanimous mission. Those sentiments were not echoed by the other white members of his party who had no horse to bear their burden.

The Indians, however, carried themselves much differently than the Virginians. Fully accustomed to relying on foot traffic for all of their travels, the Iroquois strode with a style that was upright and brisk. Their figures could not have been more of a contrast: the six-foot, four-inch frame of Washington hunched over while carefully negotiating his steed through the sharp brush and the Indians moving fluidly across the wild landscape. The Iroquois and Gist all agreed that a stop at nearby Mingotown should be made for small supplies and word of any potential reconnaissance. Their day had been short but it would be a welcomed rest.

In the modern perspective, the expedition loosely followed the Ohio River until reaching Mingotown, a small village situated at what is now Conway, Pennsylvania. While Conway is presently divided geographically by elevation, with more homes resting on top of the hill and many small houses and shops sitting at the bottom, the low-lying region near the river would have been Mingotown's original position.

With no news to report, the men departed from Mingotown and continued their northbound hike. Though their journey is largely unknown, the convoy would have most likely followed the Venango Trail, a path most familiar to their Indian allies. If traveling along Route 228 westbound into Cranberry, Pennsylvania, joy riders can make note of the blue Pennsylvania Historical and Museum Commission (PHMC) marker noting the approximate location of the Venango Trail. The general region of present-day Cranberry would have certainly been part of their journey.

The sun was beginning to set on the multicultural, multiethnic, multinational expedition, and resting for the night was on everyone's mind, most notably Washington's. For all of his travels, Gist had very little experience this far north of the Forks of the Ohio. He was well aware of his inexperience and was certainly willing to concede to the judgment of Tanacharison and his men. Their camp, the Half-King decided, would be made just north at the small collection of villages known as Murderingtown, and no one disagreed.

Murderingtown remains as one of the great mysteries of Washington's 1753 mission. Although the location of the place is not nearly as significant as understanding what occurred there, many pseudoscholars will argue with a heated fervor about the actual geographic setting of the town. The best evidence left behind is the eighteenth-century maps that generally place it in the same region, along the Connoquenessing Creek connecting modern-day Evans City, Pennsylvania, to Harmony, Pennsylvania. Washington's first experience in Murderingtown was uneventful, and its most significant legacy was the long night's rest that it provided to him. The major wrote in his journal that the trek from Logstown to Murderingtown occurred "without anything remarkable happening but a continued series of bad weather." His next visit to the unassuming village, however, would change—and nearly end—his life.

DECEMBER 1–3, 1753: THE SMALL HOURS

Washington had grown accustomed to small doses of daily excitement on their mission so far, but the thrills of diplomacy seemed to have disappeared along with the month of November. The men left Murderingtown early on December 1 and continued on through the forests and streams of western Pennsylvania. To the Virginians, their surroundings were nameless, faceless and repetitive. The tall, barren trunks of the massive trees created a maze of wilderness that left their heads spinning; sense of direction had disappeared with the westward current of the Ohio River days earlier. On the contrary, the Indians were quite familiar with this land; it was a path that they had navigated many times while venturing north.

Gist was inspired by their instinctive sense of direction; he, too, considered himself a man of the forest, but nature's less endearing elements were beginning to get the best of him. When the force departed Murderingtown earlier that morning, the skies remained dismal and still, but before long the rain came. It seemed like fate, a potentially terrible omen bestowed on a potentially doomed mission. The day was uneventful, but it certainly took its toll on the young Washington. The Virginians and Indians elected to set up camp "at the crossing of Beaver Creek from Kaskuskies to Venango, about thirty miles." They were at the current position of Slippery Rock Creek.

The northern route taken by the men has been considered to be similar to the orientation of present-day Route 19. Their departure from Murderingtown would have likely taken them through modern-day Portersville, Pennsylvania, and then to the vicinity of Muddy Creek. From Muddy Creek the team would have continued to travel at an eastward trajectory until passing through West Liberty, Pennsylvania. Their ultimate destination for the day, and site of their overnight camp, was at Crolls Mills.

The rain continued well into December 2, and all agreed that the combination of cold weather and drizzling rain would spell disaster for both the expedition and their horses. With camp already established, the Indians took to the forest for food. Although he had done away with the traditional bow and arrow methods of his ancestors, the powerful Guyasuta relished the opportunity to hunt openly. Living in villages allowed for a certain apathy to emerge, as food was generally available (though rarely plentiful), but now killing was a matter of sustenance. He was assigned the position of Hunter in the party, and it was not a title that he regarded as ceremonial.

Guyasuta waited patiently with his musket gripped tightly to his shoulder, the rain cascading down his bare forehead. Every sound of the forest served a purpose, every snapping twig sent a message and the Hunter was receptive to all of it. Out of the brush appeared a buck, and Guyasuta wasted little time appreciating his aim.

There followed a sizzle, a click and an explosion. After the blast of smoke from the igniting powder had dissipated, the large animal lay dying on the ground. The Hunter's adrenaline rushed with a familiar mixture of excitement and relief. The expedition would eat well that night.

Guyasuta would kill another buck before returning to camp.

Chapter 4

RESTRAINT

First Encounters with the French

DECEMBER 3, 1753

The meal provided by Guyasuta and his Indian allies the day before served as more than a gesture of goodwill. As the group consumed their meal, they did so as one. Through the use of interpreter John Davidson, the men shared stories of their travels, the Indians recollected past achievements and Gist corroborated them. Washington had little to add to these proceedings, as this was his first true mission of merit, but he did take the time to describe the crystal blue waters of Barbados that he had seen in his youth. The Indians appeared genuinely intrigued.

After a cold and wet night's sleep, the men arose with stiff joints and frigid prospects of the new day's journey that lay ahead of them. Unlike the bounty enjoyed by the human members of the expedition, there was relatively little sustenance for the party's horses, and the beasts could only nourish themselves by dragging their tired hooves into the dense snow and rummaging for small grasses. They most of all would need their strength; it would be their labors that allowed the convoy to move forward.

The team next continued their northward march through the wilderness. The indication given by those who kept journals reveals little information, mostly due to their comparative lack of knowledge regarding the region, but enough that historians can suggest a possible route. With Venango (Franklin, Pennsylvania) being their next destination, it can be inferred that

Unbeknownst to all in 1753, the rich supplies of coal that existed under the forests of western Pennsylvania would drive steel production in the future and help to define a city. Station Square mural. *Courtesy of the author.*

the men passed through present-day Harrisville, Pennsylvania, en route to establishing their next night's camp on Wolf Creek. Gist noted that this distance was about twenty-two miles.

December 4, 1753

The shared encampment that the team used was not dissimilar from the style used the previous nights. To tear it down and pack it in a neat and orderly fashion became routine for the force. Washington, in his youthful exuberance, had considered his journey quite extensively before it began one month earlier, but it was these small, time-consuming maintenance activities for which he hadn't prepared himself.

Spirits were high among the expedition on December 4; the Indian village of Venango was less than fifteen miles away, and Venango meant rest *indoors*. This break was sorely needed, and in fact it could not have come any sooner. The men were beginning to succumb to the elements around them, and the Virginians were trekking in a line that was a chorus of coughs, sneezes and groans. The icy rain turned their animal skin and woolen clothing into a heavy, frozen encasement causing their body temperature to drop by the minute. The Indians appeared to be quite tolerant of the wintery conditions, but they, too, were feeling its effects—they were just more accustomed to hiding their grievances.

Washington was in a daze. Trees and streams flashed by his passive senses, and he stared mindlessly forward, hypnotized by the rise and fall of the horse beneath him. With his Indian allies in tow, Washington no longer had to serve as the vigilant leader of the party. He was just as lost as his men were, and the Iroquois navigators had his blind allegiance so long as they were still in the forests. His trance was snapped rather quickly, however, upon the appearance of smoke in the distance.

It was not just a single plume of smoke that excited Washington and his men; it was the unmistakable appearance of many fires. Dozens of small pillars of ash rose from the horizon, indicating fires of different sizes, each serving a different purpose. It was not a random collection of settlers or encampments, it was a village. It was Venango.

Washington wrote about the current status of their position: "This is an old Indian Town, situated at the Mouth of French Creek on Ohio, and lies near N. about sixty Miles from Logstown, but more than seventy the Way we were obliged to go." Some interesting details can be revealed about Washington's assessment of their location. He noted that the village was located at the mouth of French Creek and the Ohio. This is an inaccurate statement but only in name. The Ohio River emerges as the result of the confluence two others, the Monongahela to the south and the Allegheny to the north. This river is actually the Allegheny and not the Ohio. Washington also claimed that the team was now sixty miles north of Logstown and yet their journey was to be seventy miles. This accounted for the detour westward to Mingotown that the team had to make in order to connect with the Venango Trail.

Washington was well aware of Venango's reputation as he and his men entered the village. This was not just an Indian village or an isolated outpost; it contained one of the largest French presences in all of the Ohio Country. The impact of daily interaction with Europeans was unmistakable. The natives of the village were of a mixed population similar to that of Logstown, and peoples of all nations were present. Mingos, Shannoahs, Iroquois and Delawares all inhabited the village. As representatives of the British Crown, though largely unnoticed upon arrival, the Virginians knew that discretion would be essential to continuing their mission.

The Indians informed Washington and Gist that their best course of action would be to consult the French Indian ambassador to the region. Washington knew of this man from the Half-King's previous stories: Captain Phillipe-Thomas Chabert de Joncaire. Joncaire had been a fixture in Washington's memory since first receiving word that he had announced to the native peoples that the French would be at the Forks of the Ohio by spring. Joncaire also received the first warning from the Indians to abandon all French possessions on that same occasion. Joncaire was a monumental figure in European-Indian relations within the Ohio Country, and Washington would meet him face to face. For the first time in his career, Washington would confront a French official in the name of Great Britain.

DIPLOMACY UNDER THE INFLUENCE

Though Venango would be the future site of Fort Machault, Joncaire himself would not be found in any such fortification; his location was much more *civilized*. Located in a more remote part of the village was the former cabin of English settler John Fraser. Fraser had been a well-known Indian trader, famous for being one the first Europeans to successfully establish a settlement west of the formidable Allegheny Mountains. Upon France's arrival in the Ohio Country, Fraser was promptly forced out of his cabin and removed from the area in a symbolic display of power. It was above this cabin that the French flag now flew and within it that Captain Joncaire now resided.

The cabin itself was modest, but Washington would not allow its insignificant appearance to deter him from his duties. He, along with Gist and his fellow Virginians, approached the cabin and alerted the captain to their arrival and intentions. The old wooden door of the cabin crept open slowly, and neither Washington nor Gist knew what would be on the other side. For all of his past experience with the Indians, Gist knew that dealing with the French could be the most savage proposition of all.

Restraint

Joncaire himself answered the door, and the men were surprised at this humble act. Though he was a French representative, Joncaire had spent a large amount of his professional career in the Ohio Country, and its diplomatic eccentricities appeared to have had worn off on him. The Virginians were promptly ushered into the cabin to escape the cold, and Joncaire appeared genuinely appreciative of their company. Washington surveyed the cabin, taking mental notes. Though the cabin was constructed by an Englishman, it did not contain many clues indicating that it was now a French possession. It had been built as a protective sanctuary from harsh realities of the Pennsylvania wilderness; neither the British colors nor the fleur-de-lis had much value when confronted by this unforgiving winter.

Joncaire was not alone in the cabin, however, and Washington was careful to note that three other officers were present during this meeting. Washington began to more fully explain his intentions when Joncaire interrupted his appeal. The captain explained that though he was of high rank, he was not the man best suited to receive the major's petition. The fort north of

Guyasuta, the Hunter. Sitting atop Pittsburgh's aptly named Mount Washington, the massive bronze sculpture by artist James A. West, *Points of View*, depicts the enigmatic and fervent Indian autonomist in reflection. *Courtesy of the author.*

their current position, Joncaire explained, was the most effective location to deliver his correspondence. With that, Joncaire immediately redirected the conversation toward a much more agreeable topic: dinner.

In true diplomatic fashion, and with the seemingly endless rain outside in mind, Washington and his men accepted Joncaire's invitation to dine. He knew that there was little danger involved, as his mission was a diplomatic one and European tradition dictated that any meeting should be, first and foremost, civil. The meal was a hearty one of local goods and produce collected by both the Indians and the French. Supplies of venison, turkey, corn and bread filled the table. But it was not the food that Washington would most remember from his first meeting with the French—it was the wine: "The wine, as they dosed themselves pretty plentifully with it, soon banished the Restraint which at first appeared in their conversation, and gave a license to their tongues to reveal their sentiments more freely."

The conversation revealed by the inebriated Joncaire and his men included the following, Washington added:

> *They told me, that it was their absolute design to take possession of the Ohio, and by God they would do it; for that they were sensible the English could raise two Men for their one; yet they knew, their motions were too slow and dilatory to prevent any undertaking of theirs. They pretend to have an undoubted right to the river, from a discovery made by one LaSalle 60 Years ago; and the rise of this expedition is, to prevent our Settling on the river or waters of it, as they have heard of some families moving out in order thereto.*

The bold statements made by the French ignited a sudden fury of patriotic fervor within the young Washington. These unflattering and dismissive words were not the result of too much alcohol but rather sentiments revealed by the abuse of it, Washington felt. His blood boiled as Joncaire and his men laughed at his own visible discomfort. The major cleared his throat as he prepared to make a rebuttal, but a cutting glance from Gist reminded him that chivalry and duty still existed (in Britain, at least). Washington restored his composure and kindly thanked Joncaire for his hospitality. The captain offered the major, as head of the party, a bed for the night. He refused.

It took a meeting with a French brute in a cabin built by the hands of an Englishman to make Washington long for his small, dirty, British camp.

December 5, 1753: Masked Intentions

The first night in Venango gave Washington his first taste of traditionally European diplomacy in a world where conventional rules did not apply. They were not in London or Versailles; they were in the Ohio Country, and centuries-old customs could be compromised with something as simple as the uncorking of a cask of fermented grape juice. The major was accepting of the result, and he was intent on not allowing his next interaction with Joncaire to be so unscrupulous.

Though his newly formed party was united under the objective of French expulsion, Washington was aware that the Indians and Virginians had prior commitments to which they had to attend. Therefore, on December 5, Tanacharison informed the major that his presence, as well as the presences of White Thunder, Jeskakake and Guyasuta, was required at a council held with the Delaware sachems of Venango. The council, the Half-King

The remaining portion of West's sculpture shows Washington in open discussions with his Indian ally. Though loyal to the Half-King, Guyasuta's future in the region would be that of an insurrectionist. *Courtesy of the author.*

explained, would be held in order to collect the string of wampum requested by the absent King Shingas as per his request. Washington acknowledged the severity of the matter and likewise added that he would once again attend to Captain Joncaire as well.

Tanacharison and the other Iroquois met in the council house of the Delawares to discuss a number of issues concerning the state of Indian affairs in the Ohio Country. In truth, Tanacharison had not been fully honest with Washington when he stated that acquisition of the wampum string was the only issue to be addressed. The deliberations were likely to have been multifaceted, with special emphasis placed on those issues most pertinent to the tribes present. Topics such as Indian-European trade, village economics and supply of firearms were all to be considered. Perhaps the most pressing concern, though, was the status of natives in the emerging power struggle for the Ohio Country. Did this recent alliance with the British appear to be a promising one? Or would remaining under the flag of France be more profitable?

Following a long and productive session of debate, Tanacharison ultimately requested that the Delaware sachems bequeath the prized wampum string to his party. Unexpectedly, though, there was doubt.

Claiming that Shingas himself never sent a speech for delivery along with the string, the sachems in council claimed that they could not, by law, fulfill the Half-King's demand. Christopher Gist recounts the Delaware response: "It was true King Shingas was a great man, but he had sent no speech and…I cannot pretend to make a speech for a king." Tanacharison had little choice but to respect their decision. The Delawares were uneasy allies and a tremendous asset to the Six Nations. The decision of the reticent chiefs would not impede him from presenting his own tribal wampum to the French.

Elsewhere, at the cabin of Joncaire, Washington was finding himself in another compromising situation. Despite the drunken charade that had taken place the night before, Joncaire retained a jovial mood when discussing politics with his new guest; Washington, however, was growing tired of the captain's insincere humor. Joncaire, the major noticed, had a habit of persisting on a topic of conversation as a means of making it seem more important than it needed to be, and in this case, the topic was his Indian allies.

Washington wrote: "He affected to be much concerned that I did not make free to bring them in before; I excused it in the best Manner I was capable, and told him I did not think their Company agreeable as I heard him say a good deal in Dispraise of Indians in general." Washington revealed further: "I knew he was an interpreter and a person of very great influence among the Indians and had lately used all possible means to draw them over to their interest; therefore I was desirous of giving no opportunity that could be avoided."

Joncaire recognized the importance of maintaining an alliance with the Half-King, and he would do anything in his power to keep it. Tanacharison's presence with Washington indicated to Joncaire that the Six Nations were beginning to favor the British, but the captain's extensive history as an Indian interpreter eased his mind. He knew that the Indians' affections were not lost, and he also knew that their fresh alliance with Washington could be easily broken. Joncaire sent for Tanacharison to join him and the major in his cabin.

Washington was helpless to stop the Half-King from arriving. He had done his best to dissuade the captain from calling for him, but Joncaire was much too intelligent to relent. He would now have to sit and watch as his new alliance with Tanacharison faced its first true test. Washington and Joncaire had run out of things to say to each other. It was yet another setback that the young major had to endure in his first weeks as a diplomat. The opening of the door and the cold chill that accompanied it startled Washington, and the ruckus of cheerfulness that followed made his stomach turn.

"Nitachinon!" they joyously called over and over again; Washington recognized this as the name given to Joncaire by the Iroquois. The captain's close relationship to the Indians of Washington's team was undeniable, but the major had no idea how much affection they really had for him. Born in Montreal in 1707, Joncaire had lived his entire life in the New World. His father had a close relationship with the native Senecas of New York, and he had quite literally grown up around Iroquois customs and traditions. Due to his fluency in the Iroquoian tongue, he eventually took a position as Indian agent for the French government. Since his assignment as interpreter in the Ohio Country, Joncaire had been a personal friend and ally to many of the sachems in the region.

The informal three-nation council that developed was unlike any that Washington had seen before involving the Indians who accompanied him.

Like the day before, the French overindulged in the pleasures of sweet wines and spoke freely about their intentions to conquer the whole of the Ohio Country. The young major understood their free willingness to intoxicate themselves in his presence—he was a fellow European, very much of the same moral standards of Joncaire and his men—but the presence of Tanacharison should have restored some sense of formality. He was sorely mistaken.

Just as quickly as the French poured another glass of wine, it appeared to Washington, the Half-King was equally anxious to consume it. Tanacharison doused himself over and over again with the burgundy nectar for most of the meeting and was very quickly unable to hold himself together; the Seneca soon became a drunkard. Impatient and agitated, Washington knew that Tanacharison would be unable to deliver the symbolic belt of wampum to Joncaire. Though he was wholly incapacitated by his natural intolerance to liquor, the Half-King was able to locate an opening in the steady stream of trivial pleasantries spewed forth by Joncaire enough to deliver his intended message. A fleeting grin crept over the face of the Frenchman (so quick, in fact, that only Washington's sobriety allowed him to see it), and Joncaire barely even replied to Tanacharison's warning. As quickly as the ultimatum was delivered it was washed away by another glass of fine French wine. The meeting ended as it began, with little progress made.

DECEMBER 6, 1753

The following day, Washington decided that it was best to keep his concerns to himself regarding the legitimacy of his new Indian alliance. If the French were able to sway Tanacharison with something as meaningless as alcohol, how truly strong could their bond be? Diplomacy was a game that Washington was quickly becoming more accustomed to, and his best alternative became clear: the major would wait. Waiting was not something that Washington was accustomed to doing. He considered himself a man of action, but the game of international relations was one best played with a silent voice and gracious smile.

The Half-King approached Washington and Gist near midday. His voice was rough and worn and his eyes bloodshot from the night of excess behind him. Davidson, the interpreter, quickly ran over to interpret for this unexpected meeting. Tanacharison began speaking without the expected preface of an apology.

Washington wrote, "The Half-King came to my tent, quite sober, and insisted very much that I should stay and hear what he had to say to the French. I fain would have prevented him from speaking anything until he came to the Commandant, but could not prevail." Tanacharison requested essentially for what amounted to a "do over"; he would meet for a second time with Joncaire (this time without alcohol) and deliver his nation's message and wampum appropriately. Washington was immediately against the Half-King's intended plan. In the mind of the major, Captain Joncaire had already proven himself to be an ineffective and inconsequential diplomat. He certainly would not be the official most influential in the Ohio Country, and their message was too vital to be lost on a lower-level French bureaucrat.

Though very different from most contemporary interpretations, this twenty-foot mural of Guyasuta graces Pittsburgh's Station Square as an homage to his importance in the region. *Courtesy of the author.*

If Washington was to take part in another summit with a French official, he decided, it would be only with the commandant of Fort Le Boeuf himself.

Tanacharison nevertheless reminded Washington that certain rules did apply in the realm of Indian affairs that were not traditionally a part of European practice: "He told me, that at this place [Venango] a council fire was kindled, where all their business with these people [the French] was to be transacted, and that the management of Indian affairs was left solely to Monsieur Joncaire." The major was frustrated by the Half-King's insistence but acknowledged the inflexibility of the situation. It was not his place to determine how other representative nations exercised their respective business, and he supported Tanacharison's decision. The meeting would take place, Washington noted, at about ten o'clock in the morning.

This was a pivotal moment in the expedition, and Washington believed that the result would greatly affect its future. If Joncaire acted appropriately, the Virginians decided, he would be forced to refuse the message and refer them to his superior at Fort Le Boeuf. It was then that the expedition would reach its desired destination and be able to complete its intended mission. If Joncaire refused to refer them and simply accepted the message himself, however, then more drastic means would be required; Washington prayed that Joncaire would refer them to Fort Le Boeuf. In preparation for their expected journey, Washington assigned that members of his party and, most importantly, his horses move ahead of them. The gamble was a calculated one: if Washington and his Indian allies were held up any

This image of Washington, which sits adjacent to that of Guyasuta in Station Square, portrays an elder statesman. *Courtesy of the author.*

longer at Venango, he risked losing those sent forward. However, if Joncaire requested that the Virginians go to Le Boeuf, then his men and horses would be well positioned and fully rested.

The critical summit with Captain Joncaire was one like Washington had never seen before. As a delegate of the British empire, the major had little voice in the matter, but he was just one of many peoples represented. The village of Venango was quite similar to that of Logstown, only on a much larger scale. While Logstown developed because of its central location to both the Ohio River and Venango Trail, Venango's already-present population grew following the rumor of the future establishment of the French Fort Machault. Therefore, when the Half-King informed Washington that a council fire would be held at the site, he truly had no choice but to issue his warning then and there.

Joncaire, like Washington, was one of many nations present at the council, but he was accompanied by a small party of fellow French aides. Unlike the previous evenings, when the Captain was careless and sloppy, tonight he was somber and attentive. Joncaire was an expert in Indian negotiations; he had spent his whole life around the native peoples of North America and was well aware of the significance of the evening's council fire.

Tanacharison, too, was of a much different demeanor than the previous night. He was no longer a smiling and lighthearted character; tonight his expression was one of stone. Washington was unsure of how the Half-King would present himself to the French and still manage to retain a sense of earnestness after his earlier, unflattering actions at Joncaire's cabin. He did not have to wait long for an answer.

Tanacharison stood proudly and delivered his message with grace and severity. It was at that moment that the major understood that the previous night's encounter was a social one, a meeting of old friends after nearly three months apart. Joncaire was now attentive, and when the Half-King handed him the symbolic wampum on behalf of the collective Indian peoples, a deafening silence engulfed the ranks of the summit; it seemed as though even the fire itself stood at attention and softened its incessant crackling. Washington held his breath as Joncaire accepted and admired the string of shells; it felt like an eternity until the captain spoke.

Joncaire had not impressed Washington as a particularly able diplomat, but at that moment his opinion of the captain was changing for the better. Joncaire had expected the message, and the wampum was typical of a warning such as this, but a man of his position was not able to properly

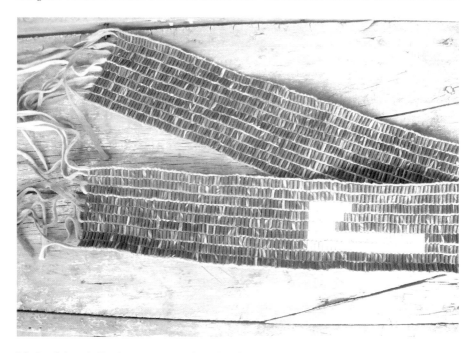

Made of tiny shells, the wampum string played an integral role in Indian diplomacy throughout the New World. *Courtesy of the Old Stone House Museum.*

process the request. He knew this, Tanacharison knew this and Washington in his greenness only hoped for this. Joncaire responded in kind by explaining that he could not receive this petition and that only a meeting with the commandant of Fort Le Boeuf would be appropriate. Tanacharison accepted his refusal with grace, and Joncaire explained that a small French convoy would accompany the Half-King, Washington and their mission northward toward the fort. Washington's stomach fluttered with excitement as he saw his plans coming to fruition.

Like a game of chess, the young major's gamble was validated: he would get his meeting with the commandant of Fort Le Boeuf, Jacques Legardeur de Saint-Pierre. In just four days, destiny awaited the twenty-one-year-old George Washington, but so did some of the harshest weather that the Pennsylvania winter had yet offered.

Chapter 5

RESOLVE

Showdown at Fort Le Boeuf

DECEMBER 10, 1753

After four days of travel, Washington was very tired. The weather was a relentless combination of snow and rain, and the streams that meandered through the Pennsylvania landscape became instantly formidable. Once passable waterways flooded and froze as staunch and unforgiving reminders of what lay ahead of the young major. But they, like the many peoples and places behind him, paled in comparison to what stood in front of him now. By the count of Christopher Gist, they had traveled nearly sixty miles since Venango, and in front of them now was the mighty Fort Le Boeuf. The fort, by all indications, was a relatively modest one compared to some of the other giants utilized by the French military, but the inexperienced Washington took careful note of its physicality nevertheless:

> *It is situated on the South, or West Fork of French Creek, near the Water, and is almost surrounded by the Creek, and a small Branch of it which forms a Kind of an island; four houses compose the sides; the Bastions are made of Piles driven into the Ground, and about 12 feet above, and sharp at Top, with Port Holes cut for Cannon and Loop Holes for the small Arms to fire through.*

The sun was setting behind the wooden structure, and the sharpened spikes that surrounded it impressed themselves on Washington's fragile

Markers like this one, created by the Washington's Trail Committee, promote local awareness of the major's travels in the Pittsburgh region and retrace the route of his 1753 journey. *Courtesy of the author.*

psyche. He had ventured hundreds of miles in this unforgiving wilderness, and every step, every alien handshake and every frigid moment was leading to this. The emotion was beginning to overwhelm him, and it became harder to conceal his anxiety as every new day passed.

Since leaving Venango on December 7, Washington and his men had become familiar with French attitudes in the Ohio Country, and as they departed days before, Joncaire insisted that they be escorted by four French officers on their journey. Washington and Gist recognized this as an inconvenience, but a knowledgeable presence was a precious commodity in these weather conditions. Leading them was Michel Pépin, a man known by his comrades as "La Force"; his persistent professionalism and unwillingness to be stifled by the cold was indication enough to Washington as to why he was given this moniker.

These Frenchmen were not an entirely welcome addition to Washington's expedition, and the strains of their subterfuge were taking toll on the major. From their final moments at Venango to their current situation, the French officers had been almost constantly attempting to dislodge the Half-King and his men from Washington's company. The Virginians watched in perpetual frustration as, time and again, Joncaire's men offered the Indians gifts of weapons and alcohol; the Iroquois always accepted.

Scholars will agree that the native peoples of the Ohio Country were masters of diplomacy and were well aware of tensions between the British and French. In turn, not unlike children of a family separated by divorce, the Indians would often play the sides off each other to achieve greater rewards for themselves. This tactic was manifesting itself, in a small way, on Washington's expedition.

Upon arrival to Fort Le Boeuf, it was "La Force" who instructed the Virginians to remain in place while he alerted the commandant to their presence. Cold, tired and ever weakening, Washington had no choice but to oblige. Gist and his old friend, Barnaby Currin, still very much part of the expedition, shot each other inquisitive glances. They had plenty of experience dealing with Indians, but the affairs of the French were not part of their repertoire.

Pépin returned shortly after and signaled them to enter. The wooden gates of Fort Le Boeuf opened slowly. Washington was shaken by the prospects of what lay ahead. Gist wrote of their greeting, "They received us with a great deal of complaisance."

DECEMBER 11, 1753: WAITING

Washington did not acquire an audience with the commandant as quickly as he had hoped. The major and his men arrived at the fort late on December 10, and after being granted room and board by the French, it quickly became apparent that December 11 would slip by without the meeting that Washington so badly desired. The delay, though anything but ideal, gave the Virginians the opportunity to recover from their frigid journey. Gist and Currin discussed potential routes by which to return south, as well as the distinct possibility that their horses might not be healthy enough to make another extended hike. Washington used his time to wisely take note of the previous days' events and mentally prepare himself for what would be the most significant moment of the entire mission.

The man he would be addressing was Jacques Legardeur de Saint-Pierre, a knight of the prestigious French military order of St. Louis and an

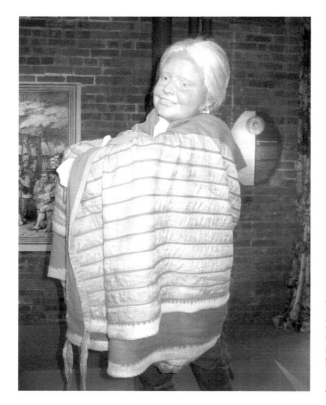

A replica of a young European girl adorned in Indian dress. Works like this one are indicative of the dichotomy existing between the two cultures. *Courtesy of the Senator John Heinz History Center.*

experienced, lifelong soldier. Saint-Pierre had been a man of prominence in French North America for some time, but it was only within the month before Washington's arrival that he had assumed total control of the outpost. He became commandant upon the death of his predecessor, the aforementioned Pierre Paul Sieur de Marin. In his naiveté, Washington, who fancied himself a military man as well, pictured himself and Saint-Pierre sitting and negotiating the fate of the Ohio Country as two seasoned officers. It made no difference to the major that he had only earned his commission weeks earlier. The major drifted off to sleep accompanied solely by the scream of the cold wind that wrapped itself around the fort.

Britain and France were the two most powerful nations on earth at this time. Their empires spanned five continents, but both now cowered in the face of the harsh Pennsylvania winter. The steady fall of snow and sleet outside served to remind them of that.

December 12, 1753: The Man and the Moment

Washington rose from his quarters as a determined man on December 12. To those in his expedition, Fort Le Boeuf was the final stop on a long and arduous journey, but they were aware of its significance. To Washington, it was the moment to which his whole twenty-one-year-old life had been leading. His men were busy packing, and Gist was directing their actions. The Indians of the party, though, had appeared to have lost sight of their mission, Washington believed. The Half-King was quite content to experiment with and tally the French gifts that he had received, and the sachems who joined him were equally captivated. Even the hunter Guyasuta, the guarded Indian nationalist, seemed enamored of the new weapons and supplies.

Despite the disorder around him, Washington was still counting down the moments until his believed date with destiny.

It was early in the day when Washington heard a knock at his door. Awaiting him was a French officer who, by his appearance, was second in command at the fort. The Frenchman led the major and Gist to the

A later depiction of Fort Le Boeuf gives some insight into what Washington saw upon his arrival. *From the* Report of the Commission to Locate the Sites of the Frontier Forts of Pennsylvania, *1895.*

commandant's lodge. It, like many of the structures inside the fort, was a simple wooden structure designed in haste with an emphasis on practicality; there was little place for pageantry in the Ohio Country. As he made his way to the chamber door, Washington became instantly aware of his own ragged appearance. He had worn the same series of garments since leaving Logstown and feared that his dismal appearance may have taken something away from his diplomatic effectiveness. Thoughts like these had flooded his mind and made him restless throughout the mission.

Washington peered inside the cabin, attempting to register as much as possible from the small space. Though he was greeted immediately by the officers within, in an instant the major noted the overwhelming darkness of the room and the futile efforts of the small fires trying to light it. He saw seated at a wooden desk an aging man in his early fifties, clearly worn from being posted in a region so desolate. His hair was gray, and his uniform contained certain features designed to display his rank—it was a gesture lost in such an untamed setting. Washington recognized this man as Commandant Saint-Pierre. The major approached the Frenchman with a sense of duty, and Saint-Pierre's expression indicated that the onus of speech would fall on the twenty-one-year-old first. Washington presented his credentials and stated his intentions.

There was no immediate response from the commandant. In this distant land, while serving as an agent of France, Saint-Pierre had become accustomed to many of the different native groups and spoke several of their languages. At the age of fifty-two, there was seldom a man more qualified for the position than he. The commandant was well suited for the task of Indian relations, but on this day one of his greatest inadequacies revealed itself to Washington: Saint-Pierre spoke almost no English.

The men surrounding the commandant indicated to Washington and Gist that they must wait for the arrival of Pierre-Jean-Baptiste-Francois-Xavier Legardeur de Repentigny, the commander of Fort Presque Isle on Lake Erie. Monsieur Reparti, as Washington wrote in his journal, was expected later in the day. It was upon his arrival, and *only* upon his arrival, that Washington should deliver his now precious letter containing the warning written by Lieutenant Governor Dinwiddie on behalf of King George II.

When comparing the journal entries of Washington and Gist, there is some discrepancy regarding the arrival of Repentigny. Washington indicated that he arrived at Fort Le Boeuf at two o'clock in the afternoon on December 12, while

Domain of Three Nations, artist John Buxton's re-creation of Washington's meeting with French officials at Fort Le Boeuf. Note the presence of Indian shadows crawling across the floor. *Courtesy of John Buxton.*

Gist does not mention the commandant's arrival until December 13. Regardless, Washington continued in his journal: "At 2 o' clock the Gentleman that was sent for arrived, when I offered the Letter, etc. again: which they received, and adjourned into a private Apartment for the Captain to translate, who understood a little English; after he had done it, the Commander desired I would walk in, and bring my interpreter to peruse and correct it, which I did."

Alongside two of the most prominent French military officials in all of the North America, the untested Washington recited the details of the letter that he considered to be of great consequence in the simplest terms possible. As though he was explaining it to a group of schoolchildren, Washington read the letter slowly, and both sides grappled with the realities of a distant language gap. The Frenchman requested a night to review the proposal, and the exhausted Washington returned to his quarters.

The task and duty that the young major had prepared for over three months had turned out to be more of a lesson in grammar and English than an exercise in diplomacy.

December 13, 1753: Reconnaissance

Awaiting an answer from Saint-Pierre seemed like an eternity. As morning slowly transformed into midday, Washington paced the floor of his cabin, and afternoon soon became evening. It was astonishingly clear, even to the inexperienced Washington, that any response from the commandant would not be made that day. The Frenchmen had mentioned at the conclusion of their summit the previous evening that they would begin a traditional council of war to discuss Lieutenant Governor Dinwiddie's demands. The wait was taking its toll on the major.

To accompany the general emotional strain of idling at an enemy position, Washington was becoming increasingly aware that his Indian comrades were conspicuously absent. Though he could not keep track of the Half-King and his fellow sachems at all times, the major had been informed by his own men that they would often disappear. They never failed to return full of conversation and with new gifts, being sure to remain out of earshot of the interpreter Davidson. Gist and Washington were distressed by these new developments and prepared themselves for the reality that the French would stop at nothing to gain the Indians' favor.

Washington was never one to rest easy; it was a virtue that would define his military and political career ahead. He ordered his team to compile a detailed tally of just how many men and canoes Fort Le Boeuf had at its disposal: "There are an hundred exclusive of Officers, of which there are many. I also gave orders to the people that were with me, to take an exact account of the canoes that were hauled up to convey their forces down in the spring, which they did, and told 50 of Witch Bark, and 170 of Pine, besides many others that were blocked out, in readiness to make."

If the French were going to make an attempt to claim the Forks of the Ohio at the spring thaw, they were well suited to do so.

Night fell with no response from Commandant Saint-Pierre.

December 14, 1753:
A North American Cold War

Gist and Washington were growing ever more disconcerted with the increasingly treacherous weather and took action to protect their men. Placing his faith on the word of Gist, Washington ordered a small convoy to abandon the fort and maneuver the expedition's horses south to Venango. This order was, like the mission itself, a gamble of the highest order. This was not to be a duty taken lightly, and the major placed Barnaby Currin at its head. Washington decided that without his horses, he would return south via the icy waters of the Allegheny River.

Currin received strict instructions to move directly and swiftly to Venango, taking care to preserve as many horses as possible. They would be sent without loads on their sore backs. Once safely at Venango, Currin was to "wait our arrival, if there was a prospect of the river's freezing; if not, then to continue down to…the forks of Ohio." It was a difficult position, and in the eyes of Gist and Washington, Currin was the only one (aside from Gist himself) capable of making such a choice. His horses were swiftly deteriorating, but equine fortitude was the least of his worries.

Just minutes before Washington's men departed, the Half-King and his allies had entered the cabin of the commandant. Tanacharison had been campaigning for an audience with Saint-Pierre since the expedition's arrival, but he had been relegated due to the presence of their British allies. Washington knew that the Half-King should be presenting the string of wampum at that moment, but after witnessing how the French had showered the Indians with gifts in previous days he was not taking any chances. The solidification of an alliance was just as plausible as the conclusion of one.

The Half-King concluded his council with the commandant and did not carry the look of a man who had just created an enemy. To avoid any suspicion and protect his dignified image, Washington allowed Tanacharison to approach him with the results. The Half-King explained that he did, in fact, deliver the wampum as planned but that Saint-Pierre refused to acknowledge it. Over and over again, Tanacharison introduced his people's message, and the commandant spoke only of the good relationship that the French and Iroquois had fostered over many months. Saint-Pierre promised nothing to the Half-King but many years of friendship and prosperous trade;

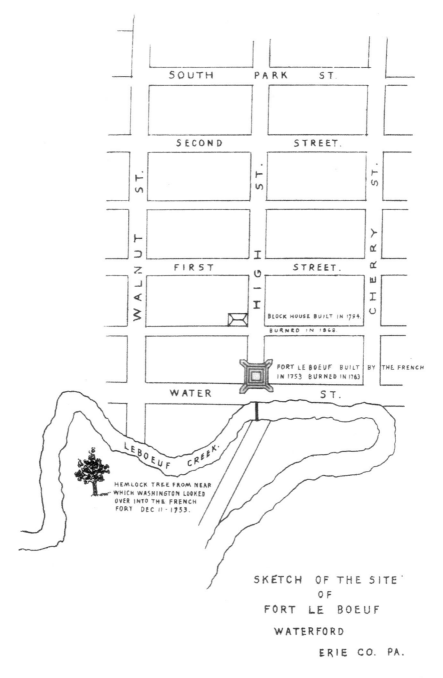

SKETCH OF THE SITE
OF
FORT LE BOEUF
WATERFORD
ERIE CO. PA.

This sketch shows the relative location of Fort Le Boeuf overlaid with a later map of Waterford, Pennsylvania. *From the* Report of the Commission to Locate the Sites of the Frontier Forts of Pennsylvania, *1895.*

he even went so far as to pledge that a shipment of goods would be delivered to Logstown upon their arrival as a show of good faith. The commandant implored the Half-King to remain at Le Boeuf after the Virginians had left, and Washington suspected that a French officer would most likely be assigned to accompany them. These promises troubled the major; if the French were willing to open a permanent supply line to Logstown, that meant that many English traders in the region would be, quite literally, left out in the cold. Jacques Legardeur de Saint-Pierre was waging a North American cold war that would soon turn hot.

Though Washington had not yet heard from the commandant, he was able to acquire the ear of Monsieur Reparti. The major was troubled by the outcome of Tanacharison's council and sought answers courtesy of the commander's grasp of the English language. Washington was not so bold, or foolhardy, as to inquire about the proceedings of the Half-King's meeting, but he was curious as to how the French meant to explain other issues that had caused tension in recent months. Washington was rattled by recent developments, and assuming the role of pseudointerrogator was not easing his troubled spirit. The topic of conversation regarded the recent capture and detention of loyal British subjects by French militia. Washington had heard rumors that a young boy was recently taken into custody and seen at Fort Le Boeuf, but Reparti claimed to have no knowledge of it. Washington expected as much.

The major was not so willing to accept that Reparti was ignorant to the plights of John Troter and James McLocklin. Troter and McLocklin were British traders living and operating in the Ohio Country; they were arrested by French Infantry and seldom seen or heard from again. Reparti halfheartedly acknowledged that he had seen the men, but he claimed that they had been promptly taken to Canada and returned home. He concluded their conversation by stating plainly that "the Country belonged to them [the French], that no Englishman had a right to trade upon those waters; and that he had orders to make every person prisoner that attempted it on the Ohio, or the waters of it."

Whatever the anticipated response of Saint-Pierre was, Washington was growing more and more certain that it would not involve any French concession of the Ohio Country.

A Cordial Response

Washington wasted no time in sharing the details of his conversation with Gist; with their original expedition now venturing southward, the men were more dependent on each other than ever before. It was approaching dusk, and Washington began to consider that perhaps the commandant was intentionally keeping him in waiting.

Washington was admittedly new to diplomacy, but such a tactic was taking a definite psychological toll on him. He had envisioned the delivery of Dinwiddie's letter dozens, even hundreds, of times in his mind, but none of the previous manifestations ever included a two-day wait for a response. Suddenly there was a shuffling outside of his cabin door—and voices.

The words were in French, indistinguishable to Washington himself, but the voice was undeniable: it was Saint-Pierre.

The banging at the door signified to the major that it was time for an official decision. Following his earlier conversation with Monsieur Reparti, Washington was prepared for a verbal show of force. Today he was not just a young officer from Virginia, he was not the brother of Lawrence Washington and he was not simply a colonist. The twenty-one-year-old was a representative of King George himself, and he was prepared to defend his country's honor. His mind was flooded with scenarios and potential responses in the short walk from his bunk to the cabin door, and upon opening it he realized that he had no idea what to expect.

Standing firmly, despite the frigid temperatures and blustering wind, was Commandant Saint-Pierre and a small party of officers; Monsieur Reparti was in tow. Washington greeted the men with a stone face, a miraculous feat considering the adrenaline that was coursing through his body. He stood with his hands clasped behind his back to disguise the tremors that rendered them useless, and he welcomed in his hosts. Decades of battle and blood feud between France and Britain were, in the mind of Washington, playing out directly in front of him at a small outpost seated thousands of miles from Europe. With a deep breath, the major opened his tightly pursed lips to speak.

The commandant smiled and spoke first. With all the grace and poise of a lifelong servant of France, Saint-Pierre handed Washington a sealed letter. It was explained to the major that it contained a response and should be returned with all expediency to Lieutenant Governor Dinwiddie.

Washington was taken aback. There was no tension and no confrontation—the commandant's response was offered simply as a gesture of good faith. The officers who accompanied Saint-Pierre expressed that whatever supplies Washington desired would be provided free of charge. The commandant tipped his hand to the young major and left him for the night. Washington was left holding the letter delivered by the Frenchman, amazed at the level of composure and elegance by which it was handed over. How could a man of such high military standing, a man who had opposed Britain his entire professional career, remain so polished? The major realized that, of all of his adventures and experience gained thus far, he had much to learn.

In his bunk for the night, Washington struggled to come down from the emotional hurricane that raged inside of him. The torrid mix of feelings—anger, rage, duty, fear and more—had begun to settle and gradually disappear. His eyelids grew heavy, his mind at rest. He had a long journey home ahead of him, and he hoped to leave in the morning.

As sleep finally began to embrace Washington, he was surprised to discover that, among all others, he had only one true sentiment for the commandant: respect.

December 15, 1753: "I Could Not Say that Ever in My Life I Suffered So Much Anxiety"

The following morning, Washington was pleased to see that the commandant had lived up to his word. The team's canoes, which were located outside of the fort along with the larger French supply, were being steadily filled with provisions of liquor, supplies and foodstuffs. It was an interesting spectacle to the major. The commandant was doing everything possible to ensure that Washington and Gist would have a safe journey home, but he maintained a distance, a unique coldness that served as a reminder that they were on opposing sides of a historic conflict. Saint-Pierre was the overseer of the daily affairs of Fort Le Boeuf, and his attention was divided between those and the task of resupplying Washington and Gist. These kind acts, however, were part of a larger scheme, and Washington was quick to recognize the dualistic nature of diplomacy of this order, for even as the commandant was giving he was also attempting to take from them as well.

After days of gift-giving and flattery, Tanacharison and his men were quickly becoming quite fond of the French, as noted in Washington's journal: "Presents, rewards, and everything that could be suggested by him or his Officers—I can't say that ever in my life I suffered so much anxiety as I did in this affair; I saw that every stratagem that the most fruitful brain could invent, was practiced, to win the Half-King to their interest, and that leaving him here was giving them the opportunity they aimed at."

Washington was now in a panic. While he had been merely aggravated by the Frenchmen's movements toward the Indians earlier, he was becoming alarmed that the Iroquois were now an asset on the verge of being lost. The major was bewildered and brushed past the infantrymen loading his supplies; he was in a desperate search to distance the Half-King as much as possible from Saint-Pierre and his men. The snow crunched beneath his feet as Washington interrupted the proceedings: "I went to the Half-King, and pressed him in the strongest terms to go: He told me the Commandant would not discharge him 'til the morning."

The major was angry, and after completing the primary objective of his mission, he had seen enough. Washington rushed over to the commandant and confronted the Frenchman. Saint-Pierre's underhanded ruse had been revealed, and he made no attempt to keep it hidden from Washington. He openly attempted to sway Tanacharison, and the young Virginian's blood boiled. Rules of civility and rank did not apply at this point. Washington managed to refrain from raising his voice to the commandant after regaining some composure, but he did not soften his harsh demands:

> *I then went to the Commandant, and desired him to do their* [the Indians'] *business, and complained of ill treatment: for keeping them, as they were part of my company, was detaining me: which he promised not to do, but to forward my journey as much as he could: He protested he did not keep them, but was ignorant of the cause of their stay; though I soon found it out:—He had promised them a present of guns, etc. if they would wait 'til the morning.*

Washington was anxious to leave Fort Le Boeuf and return home on that day, but he was well aware of the consequences of doing so. Tanacharison had told the major that they would leave in the morning after receiving their gifts, and Washington was left caught in a bind. If he left now, his Indian associates were sure to remain and any alliance formed was certain to be lost. If he stayed, Tanacharison would receive his promised gifts and the Half-King would grow fonder of Saint-Pierre and France.

After weighing the consequences, Washington relented and stayed another night. He believed that it would be better to have allies who favored the French than to have no allies at all. To make matters more strenuous, he also had a time-sensitive letter—the contents of which he was blind to but believed to be incredibly important—that needed to be delivered to Lieutenant Governor Dinwiddie in Virginia. Time was of the essence, and it was a luxury that the young Washington did not have.

Washington did not open the letter destined for Dinwiddie, but he burned with curiosity to read Saint-Pierre's reply. The major soon found solace in sleep, blissfully unaware of the nature of the commandant's message. Washington was correct to assume that it was of great importance, for its contents left little doubt regarding the fate of the Ohio Country. War was on the horizon:

> *As to the summons you send me to retire, I do not think myself obliged to obey it…*
>
> *I have the honor to be,*
> *Sir,*
> *Your very humble and very obedient servant,*
>
> *Legardeur de Saint-Pierre*
>
> *From the fort on the Riviere aux Boeufs,*
> *December 15, 1753*

Chapter 6

FRAILTY

Accepting Consequences

AUGUST 2010

Located about thirty miles north of Point State Park, Evans City, Pennsylvania, stands as a testament to days gone by. Mired in antiquated simplicity, residents and visitors of Evans City take refuge in its quaint charm. While it's not exactly Mayberry, Evans City does have a way of keeping one's soul at peace. Seated a mere five miles northwest from it is the smallish city of Zelienople, a busy hub of activity in southern Butler County.

The roadway that connects the two municipalities is State Route 68—or, if so inclined, Evans City Road. Although there is nothing particularly exciting about the eight-minute journey, the history that one passes is of undeniable importance. Driving on a clear day, commuters will begin their trek by climbing a steady incline as they approach their destination. Zelienople—or "Zelie," as it is affectionately called by locals—is divided by the busy flow of traffic on Route 19, which extends well into the Pittsburgh metro area and serves as a double-edged sword for residents of the small town. On one hand, it ushered in a new wave of visitors, allowing local specialty stores and small-market museums to thrive; on the other it makes crossing Main Street much more dangerous than it used to be.

The importance of Route 19 is vital to understanding why such heavy traffic exists on Evans City Road, a veritable "road to nowhere." Though Evans City itself is not typically publicized as a must-see destination of the Pittsburgh area, it is strategically located near Interstate 79 and the aforementioned Route 19. For those in the Pittsburgh area, a visit to this charming corner is either a fond memory or part of the not-too-distant future.

All of this contributes to the line of traffic seen on Evans City Road. As one zips along the peaks and valleys of the rural highway, its ordinariness is staggering. Lumberyards, convenience stores and elementary schools make this journey simply mundane. However, following two uneventful miles, something out of the ordinary will surely turn heads. While it appears at first as a marker for the approaching on-ramp to Interstate 79 in the traditional colors of royal blue, white and red, upon closer inspection the sign will reveal itself to be quite unique. Posted on a regulation eight-foot sign post and spanning nearly thirty-six inches in diameter, the circular marker is emblazoned with a familiar shape: the profile of George Washington.

Placed by a group of civic-minded community members known as the Washington's Trail Committee, these historic reminders can be found in selected regions of western Pennsylvania deemed significant in an effort to identify the route taken by Washington during his 1753 expedition to Fort Le Boeuf.

The sign is one of many that litter the countryside to its north and south, and its presence could be forgotten—that is, until another is passed shortly thereafter. Most passengers will recognize the symbol, and many will admit to passing it every day, but only a small percentage can explain its true significance.

More than 250 years before Evans City Road graced the hills of Butler County, there existed a small confederation of Indian villages known as Murderingtown. In December 1753, on a cold and snowy winter's eve, a twenty-one-year-old version of the future president of the United States walked its streets.

Dejected, tired and defeated, the young Washington was shaken by the blast of a musket and the zing of a bullet only fifteen yards ahead. It was fired by his own treasonous Indian guide, and it was meant for him.

DECEMBER 23, 1753: A RETURN JOURNEY

It had been an arduous seven days since Washington and his party had left Fort Le Boeuf, and the Indian village of Venango was a welcomed sight; they had arrived just one day earlier. As was the case in his earlier travels with his older brother, Lawrence, in his teen years, Washington fully expected his trek southward to be a dull one. At this point, Washington had become fully accustomed to a certain level of excitement.

Though he anticipated a less difficult task, the reality of the past seven days had left a distinct aching to his large frame. Unlike their northbound trail weeks earlier, the return route had fully taken on the harsh flare of a western Pennsylvania winter. Creeks and streams, once able to be crossed rather easily, had been rendered impassible by unforgiving clusters of ice, and the expedition's horses were growing increasingly weak by the hour. After a long evening's rest at Venango, the first significant stopping point on the journey, Washington was reluctantly preparing himself to continue his wayward voyage.

This weathered statue stands today in Waterford, Pennsylvania, to commemorate Washington's cold December meeting at Fort Le Boeuf. *Courtesy of the author.*

It had been quite an adventure in Washington's eyes, but before it could continue, he reminded himself that he was, first and foremost, a diplomat. The Indians who had accompanied Washington were becoming a growing point of anxiety for the major, and a word with the Half-King was in order:

> *He told me that White Thunder had hurt himself much, and was sick and unable to walk, therefore he was obliged to carry him down in a Canoe: As I found he intended to stay here a Day or two, and know that Monsieur Joncaire would employ every scheme to set him against the English as he had before done; I told him I hoped he would guard against his Flattery, and let no fine Speeches influence him in their Favour: He desired I might not be concerned, for he knew the French too well, for any Thing to engage him in their Behalf.*

The Half-King had made his point clear: they were in no position to set out at the pace that Washington had intended. This position was unsettling to the major, and after some deliberation he conceded to the wishes of the Seneca. White Thunder had taken badly to the harsh weather, and his physical condition was deteriorating badly. Washington understood Tanacharison's position well: although his loyalties lied unsteadily to the British, the interests of his tribal brethren would always come first. Following a warning regarding the underhanded tactics of the French, to which the Half-King responded, Washington returned to his quarters to prepare for the long stretch that lay ahead.

GRIEVANCES

The recent developments with the expedition and its Indians had left suspicions high, and the inclement weather left spirits low. The travel was harsh and difficult, and any preconceived objectives regarding distance were very quickly rendered obsolete. Washington was aware of the problems that could arise by instituting the wilderness equivalent of a forced march on his men, but he saw no other option but to continue. It would not be the first time that those who joined Washington on his journey would second-guess his unproven decision-making process.

Frailty

From the beginning of their mission, the hardened frontiersmen struggled with maintaining their original objective of guiding the young major northward while being careful not to damage his fragile ego by undermining him. Among the most critical was Christopher Gist, though he rarely wrote of any open confrontation. He knew what was at stake, and he knew that it was Washington, not he, who held the key to accomplishing a successful mission and collecting a maximum bounty. Discontentment with Washington's lofty goals aside, the Virginians feebly navigated their way southward and from Venango.

After a full day's march, the men traveled a mere five miles; they would spend Christmas Eve huddled together alongside Sandy Creek in present-day Mercer County, Pennsylvania.

The next morning, after an especially uncomfortable encampment, the men of the expedition awoke at daybreak and waited for the major to emerge from his tent. As they loaded their baggage onto the emaciated and sinewy backs of their horses, Washington greeted the day in uncharacteristic fashion. Gist and the men, unprepared for the sight in front of them, stopped in momentary disbelief. For the length of the journey, the major had embraced his new title by wearing clothing that was official and, though dignified, highly impractical. On this day, however, he was dressed head to toe in a traditional Indian garb that he described as "an Indian walking dress." This was no country for diplomats, and now the major looked like a frontiersman. Humor was in short supply at this juncture, however, and the men hardly chuckled; staying ahead of the storm was vital.

Christmas Day was spent wandering through twisted thickets and winding trails, and due to the worsening conditions of their horses, the Virginians were forced to walk alongside their withered beasts. There was not much the men could offer the animals, save for bearing some of the burden of the unforgiving march.

Finally, on December 26, the Virginians watched helplessly as their horses gave out. The animals fell repeatedly on the trail, and after they spilled their payloads on numerous occasions, Washington was forced to make an executive decision. The cold wind was chilling, and a verdict was needed without the luxury of spare time for deliberation. Certainly pressed and undeniably panicked, Washington announced that the expedition would abandon the horses and continue on foot. He handed over provisions in the form of supplies and money to the members of his team and proclaimed that only Gist and himself would press forward to Virginia. The others, along with the horses, would make for the nearest settlement (whether Indian or white) and wait out the storm.

For the first time, Gist wrote, he outwardly opposed the twenty-one-year-old's announcement:

> *The Major desired me to set out on foot, and leave our company, as the creeks were frozen, and our horses could make but little way. Indeed, I was unwilling he should undertake such a travel, who had never been used to walking before this time. But, as he insisted on it, I set out with our packs, like Indians, and travelled eighteen miles.*

Tired, sore, worn and frustrated, Washington and Gist stayed the night at an available Indian cabin. For Gist, the experienced woodsman, such a trek was uncomfortable but certainly nothing new. Washington, however, spent the night staring into the emptiness of the cabin roof. His original expeditionary force of nearly a dozen was now whittled down to two. He hoped that his decision would not be a costly one.

December 27, 1753: Murderingtown

Washington and Gist elected to move early the next day, starting out at two o'clock in the morning. With the weather becoming increasingly clear, their intended goal was unknown; both men knew that Mother Nature's wintery fury could ignite at a moment's notice. Regardless of the conclusion of the day's march, Gist knew full well that the bustling Indian village of Murderingtown was not far off and that it would offer a much-needed break for the weary travelers.

One of the great mysteries of the story, and a constant point of debate among modern historians, the exact location of Murderingtown remains uncertain. However dubious its exact coordinates may be, all agree that the relative site of this lost Indian village was most certainly between Evans City and Zelienople, Pennsylvania. Nevertheless, through all of the heated debate and petty assaults on both credentials and character, the historic town of

Frailty

Harmony, Pennsylvania, now serves as an agreeable middle ground for most Washington enthusiasts.

Though they had visited Murderingtown only weeks earlier, Gist's finely tuned instincts made him suspicious of their return visit. When they arrived in the village later that day, he carefully observed the various native peoples who inhabited it. Instantly, he found what he was looking for.

Gist recognized the Indian man from his previous meetings with Captain Joncaire at Venango. Noticing Gist noticing him, the Indian came over to speak. He addressed Gist by his Indian name, Annosanah, and appeared to be overly friendly. Washington, now the experienced diplomat in full Indian regalia, graciously introduced himself to the conversation. The Indian was greatly interested in their journey to this point, a yarn that Washington proudly weaved for his one-man audience, all the while Gist was reluctant to divulge any information to his unfamiliar company.

Following more niceties between the Indian and the major, Washington indicated that he would like to return to the Forks of the Ohio as quickly as possible. It was the opening for which the Indian had been waiting. With a handshake and a smile, the Indian offered to guide the men southward toward the Forks courtesy of a little-known, but clear, bypass. He promised that it would greatly expedite their journey home.

With little hesitation, Washington accepted his offer, and though he had his doubts, Gist conceded as well. In spite of the fact that his senses had been dulled by the frigid days behind him, Gist's suspicions stayed on high alert, and they needed be: it appeared to him as though Washington's were at a new low.

IMPACT

The men took advantage of the village's provisions to rest, and shortly after their initial conversation with their new guide, they began their journey southward. The Indian, who kept a surprisingly brisk pace, led the men through the wilderness with little hesitation. As he walked, he incessantly spoke highly of British ambitions in the New World and offered time and again to carry the major's pack. Washington, originally flattered by the man's hospitality, began to doubt his sincerity. Mile after mile ticked away, and the major and Gist were becoming increasingly tired. The flatteries continued from the guide ahead, now more than ten yards in front of the Virginians. Washington did his best to hide his fatigue so as to keep his dignified appearance, but it was becoming more and more difficult not to breathe heavily. Sensing their exhaustion, the Indian offered to take the major's firearm to ease his travels.

Gist instantly froze. He knew full well that Washington could not keep at this grinding pace; he himself hardly could, and he recognized that the Indian was intentionally wearing them down. That was no secret; the look that Washington gave Gist alerted him to his awareness of the situation. It was what Washington *didn't* realize that troubled Gist: though the Forks of the Ohio were south of Murderingtown they had walked nearly ten miles to the northeast.

The men continued to trudge through the forest until Washington finally spoke up, requesting that they stop at the next stream; Gist, a subordinate, would never have asked himself, in respect to the major's senior rank. The Indian insisted that his cabin was not far and that they would arrive there before reaching any form of flowing water. They pressed reluctantly onward.

As they entered a clearing with no cabin in sight, Gist was on the verge of pulling Washington aside to inform the major as to the severity of their situation. He dropped his head down as he pressed up a small hill in the meadow, and Washington gasped. Fifteen yards ahead, the Indian had dropped to one knee, with his musket aimed directly at Washington.

With a whoop, he fired at the major; flames and rage spewed forth from the musket, and before either man could react the Indian turned and ran. Washington froze as his body reacted to the adrenaline-fueled shock of the event. He quickly began to run his hands down his torso, awaiting the bullet wound that would surely take his life in the God-forsaken landscape. He found nothing, no wound. The Indian had missed. There was no doubt, however, that the bullet was meant for him. But what of Gist? With a sudden realization of his own good fortune, he looked to Gist, certain that he was hit. To his surprise, the major turned to find his guide standing firm with his musket pointed ahead.

Gist was perfectly still. His target was sprinting away quickly, but he was still well within range. With his finger on the trigger, Gist prepared to kill his would-be assassin. In the second before he fired, he took one last breath. It was then that a hand appeared on the barrel of his cold musket—it was Washington's.

Due to the tedious effort that it took the Indian to reload his musket, Washington and Gist were able to bear down on their attacker without shooting him. As the Indian reloaded, Gist grabbed the assassin and viciously threw him to the ground. With the Indian now firmly under their control, the Virginians looked at one another for a moment and smiled—they decided to make camp for the night.

Hours later, now stripped of his weapons, tied with rope and gracious to be alive, the Indian said little to his captors. The sun was setting on the western Pennsylvania countryside.

For Gist, his prisoner's silence was no issue; he relished the opportunity to talk for both of them. The wind howled as the inquisition began, with the barren trees of the forest as the only jury at hand.

This depiction at Station Square shows Washington and Gist, now alone, peacefully navigating the Allegheny River. *Courtesy of the author.*

"I suppose you were lost and fired your gun," Gist said.

The Indian ignored the cynical indictment and remarked that his cabin was truly not far off.

"Well, do you go home; and as we are much tired, we will follow your track in the morning." Gist offered his prisoner a piece of bread. He then turned to the still shell-shocked Washington.

"As you will not have him killed, we must get him away," Gist paused. "Then we must travel all night."

Washington could do nothing but nod in agreement. So far, his decisions had only managed to compromise their mission, and that night they had almost killed him.

They soon fell asleep around the meager fire that Gist built outside of Murderingtown, and the falling snow landed gently on the forest floor. Later that night, Washington awoke to find Gist untying the man who had nearly took his life just hours earlier. The major did not sit up; he simply opened his eyes and took in the sight. As quickly as Gist had secured the stranger upon his capture he effortlessly untied the makeshift rope shackles and watched the Indian run away. He paused a moment to ensure that the man had no intention of returning.

With the assassin now only a bad memory, Gist readied his supplies. He set his mental compass southward, packed his sleeping supplies and turned to Washington, still sprawled out across the forest floor. No words were needed. They both knew that they had a long day ahead of them.

December 28, 1753

The next day was not without its excitement. Setting out from where Gist described as "the head of Piney Creek," in present-day Wexford, Pennsylvania, the men calculated that they were a little more than two miles (in reality, they were nearly fifteen miles away) from their intended destination at the Forks of the Ohio. While the previous day had left Washington badly shaken, it had made him sharper; the unique ability to sense danger that made him such a reliable frontiersman was now fully functioning.

Just as in almost every other facet of his young life, Washington spent most of the day's hike looking ahead. In contrast, Gist carefully watched the snowy forest floor below. The heavy snowfall earlier in the week had provided a thick blanket of snow, and footprints were visible in the frozen landscape. The prints, which were carefully measured, were most certainly those of an Indian hunting party, and despite the clear age of the tracks, Gist was no longer willing to take chances. He had had his fill of hostile natives with guns.

To ensure that Commandant Saint-Pierre's response was delivered, Gist and Washington agreed to part ways so that if one was attacked the other could press on. They would not separate for long and were likely to remain within earshot of each other should any incident occur. For the remainder of the day, the men walked alone, only a few hundred yards apart, and reunited for the night's camp at dusk. It was at this point that Gist scribbled a brief yet useful entry into his journal: "We encamped, and thought ourselves safe enough to sleep."

DECEMBER 29, 1753: A RIVER'S RAGE

The previous night's diligence had been unnecessary, as no attacks occurred, but Washington took comfort in Gist's deliberate measures to ensure his safety. Past events, however, were no matter, for the major prepared for what would be the day that surely would have taken them to the Forks of the Ohio and, more importantly, a bit of safety and warmth at the Indian outpost of Shannopin's Town. Located on the banks of the Monongahela River, the small outpost of Shannopin's Town sat at the present site of the parking facility known as the "Mon Wharf."

Although the weather was clear, the day was by far the coldest that they had experienced yet since leaving Fort Le Boeuf, and both Washington and Gist were praying that the mighty Allegheny River, their biggest obstacle yet, would be frozen over and passable by foot. Soon, though, their hearts sank upon seeing the Allegheny steadily babbling in front of them.

Recognizing their duty and sensing the cold increasing, the Virginians reluctantly began to seek out small trees to construct a raft. It was then that Gist realized the true folly of separating from their much larger party days earlier: they only had but one hatchet between the two of them.

For the whole of the day, from late morning until sundown, Gist and Washington took turns chopping down trees and collecting timber for their

John Buxton's *Washington's Crossing, 1753* depicts a more accurate portrayal of Washington and Gist crossing the Allegheny River moments before the former plunged into the icy current. *Courtesy of John Buxton.*

makeshift raft with their single, meager tool. Instead of a preteen Washington chopping down a proverbial cherry tree in Virginia, the scene was now, in reality, a twenty-one-year-old Washington hacking away at maples and evergreens in western Pennsylvania with a single-gripped hatchet.

As the sun set, the men, now exhausted from cutting and hewing their raft, set sail with hopes of reaching Shannopin's Town within the next hour. The river crossing, after all, was less than two hundred yards.

On unsteady legs, Washington and Gist navigated across the river in a standing position. Using leftover branches for steering, the men slowly crept across the dirty water, now dealing with treacherous ice drifts coupled with an increasing current. Both men meticulously struggled to retain their balance, but such efforts required sturdy legs and a low center of gravity; preserving either was growing noticeably difficult for the six-foot-four Washington. Gist, whose fingers and toes were now experiencing the early stages of frostbite, did his best to maintain a grip on his oar.

The next scene unfolded at a breakneck speed. As the makeshift ferry approached a small island—most likely Herr's Island beneath the present-

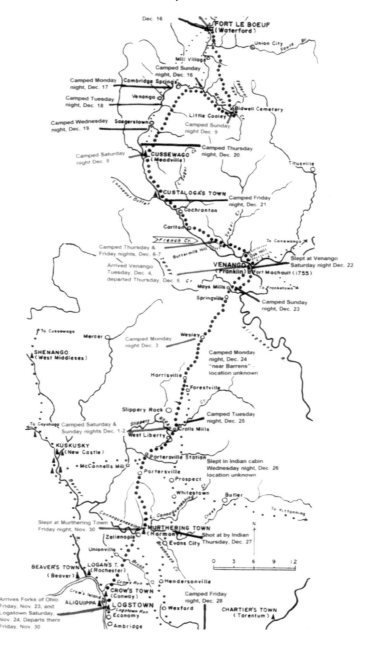

A faithful reproduction of Washington's 1753 journey, one of the many wonderful contributions by Historic Harmony, a local history advocate organization. *Mission Timeline Map © Historic Harmony Inc., which is based on a map in* Indian Paths of Pennsylvania, *Paul A. W. Wallace, Appendix V, "George Washington's Path to Fort Le Boeuf, 1753," Pennsylvania Historical and Museum Commission, Harrisburg, © 1965 and 2005, Commonwealth of Pennsylvania.*

day Thirty-first Street Bridge just north of Pittsburgh—the current beneath them began to transform into a swirling chaos of ice and dirt. Gist, positioned in the rear, wobbled as a result and could not steady the raft. In the front, however, Washington was beginning to falter due to the violent bucking of the wood below. In a sudden jolt, Gist stepped forward as the front end of the raft lifted high into the air; his rear weight was no longer balanced.

Gist watched in horror as the major flipped into the icy current with a splash; he instantly realized that for the second time in two days the young George Washington's life was in jeopardy.

Like ten thousand tiny needles, the cold washed across the body of Washington. He gasped for air in the rushing current and instantly fell into a state of shock. He struggled against the deadly pull of the river and could feel small crystals of ice developing against his eyelashes and nose. In contrast to the merciful jolt of the bullet that would have killed him instantly days earlier, Washington could now feel his life force seeping out of him by the second.

The Allegheny was not forgiving. For the first time, the young man began to realize that no future was certain, including his. He was not *owed* the life that he believed he deserved. He, too, could succumb. He thrashed violently until, miraculously, his uncommonly long arms struck the corner of the raft. He held on with what little strength remained in gaunt frame.

Gist hurriedly pulled him aboard, ignoring the searing pain in his own frostbitten hands. As the experienced man, Gist knew that Washington could not continue to Shannopin's Town, and he steered the raft to the aforementioned island and pulled the major ashore. Washington, now recovering from the shock that his body was violently thrown into, shivered and watched through blurry eyes as Gist hurried to create a fire. Any hesitancy to do so would have most likely only aided in Washington slipping deeper into hypothermia.

With a small fire now roaring valiantly, Gist replaced the Indian garb that Washington had been wearing with his previously worn diplomatic attire; wearing wet clothes would only serve to draw more precious heat from his already depleted body. Washington would sleep that night on that small island, and Gist would remain awake to keep a watchful eye on his injured comrade. The major's skin was now an unnatural blue—a stark contrast to the deep red of the officer's jacket that he wore. The colors of the British empire seemed to be anything but regal to Gist at that moment.

If traveling into the city of Pittsburgh today, southbound on Route 28, one can marvel in the fact that this impressive event took place just beneath the current site of the Fortieth Street Bridge, and despite the lack of a success in doing so, it is known today as "Washington's Crossing." "Washington's Blunder" just doesn't elicit the same response.

The night would only become colder, and Gist piled his own garments over the prone Washington. As the sun rose, Washington's condition was improving greatly, and Gist could only smile at the sight before him.

The bitter cold that had nearly killed George Washington had done them some good. The Allegheny River had frozen over. Gist, with Washington supported on his shoulder, walked ashore. The sun was rising to the east.

JANUARY 16, 1754: A JOURNEY COMPLETED

Washington sat in his chambers provided by Dinwiddie in the city of Williamsburg, Virginia. He looked out his parlor window as he scribbled a brief summary of the previous two weeks—his final two weeks of travel since nearly dying in the Allegheny River. After a brief stop at John Fraser's cabin on January 1, the men had continued to Gist's cabin at Wills Creek on January 6. It was there that Washington resupplied with enough materials and horses to allow him to arrive safely in Williamsburg sixteen days later; Gist remained in Maryland.

Though his mission was nearly a failure and fraught with disaster, this day was well worth his efforts. He made an audience with Dinwiddie and delivered the letter from Saint-Pierre with all the air of a seasoned diplomat. Influential members of the Ohio Company of Virginia all congratulated the major with well-deserved pats on the back and several informal toasts of the finest liquor in the colonies. The weight of the British empire felt as though it was back on his boastful shoulders.

Washington smiled as the people outside his temporary chamber bundled up and complained of the chill in the Virginia air. Well-dressed ladies and crisply outfitted gentlemen scurried past his window in a rush to escape the wind, and Washington laughed at his new definition of what it meant to be truly cold.

With these light thoughts in his mind, Washington beamed at the reward he was certain to receive for his efforts; though he did not know it at the time, the major would become a lieutenant colonel within months.

Now in the warm confines of home, Virginia, he opened his worn journal and added a final entry:

> [We] *arrived in Williamsburg the 16th, and waited upon his Honour the Governour with the Letter I had brought from the French Commandant, and to give an Account of the Proceedings of my Journey, which I beg Leave to do by offering the foregoing, as it contains the most remarkable Occurrences that happened to me.*
>
> *I hope it will be sufficient to satisfy your Honour with my Proceedings; for that was my Aim in undertaking the Journey, and chief Study throughout the Prosecution of it.*
>
> *With the Hope of doing it, with infinite Pleasure, subscribe myself, Your Honour's most Obedient, And very humble Servant,*
> *G. WASHINGTON*

Epilogue
LATE MARCH 1754

A s April approached, Washington admired himself in the large mobile mirror that was brought into his spacious parlor at Mount Vernon. Since his return from the Ohio Country, the *Maryland Gazette* had published the journal that he kept during the harsh winter before, and Washington's fame was beginning to overshadow his growing, yet modest, fortune.

On this day, he was trying on some newly delivered jackets. Washington's unique physical dimensions often required his clothes to be altered; after all, there weren't many customers over six-foot-four who could afford his expensive tastes. As he posed and postured, he was decidedly pleased with the tailor's work. He felt like an aristocrat—it was time he started dressing like one, too.

While twisting and turning away in his private quarters, Washington paused. His eyes locked with that of his reflected doppelganger. He remembered the fear in Gist's eyes when he himself was submerged in the icy Allegheny. He remembered the defiance in Commandant Saint-Pierre at Fort Le Boeuf. Most of all, he remembered looking into the eyes that changed his life forever.

He drifted back to a night in late December, two nights after falling into the river that almost took his life.

DECEMBER 31, 1753—Nightfall had overtaken the landscape, and Washington peered cautiously at Gist as they made their way to the cabin

A contemporary depiction of Queen Aliquippa, matriarch of the Seneca tribes in the Pittsburgh region. *Photo by author.*

of the Seneca matriarch, Aliquippa. Though Europeans would inaccurately address her as "Queen," to the Senecas of the region Aliquippa was much more than that—she was "Mother." While at Shannopin's Town, the men received word from locals that Queen Aliquippa sought their presence. They knew that they must oblige.

Aliquippa, they were told, could be found at the mouth of the Youghiogheny River, today the city of McKeesport, Pennsylvania. When the men located the small outpost, there was no doubt that the tiny village was centered on the presence of this mysterious woman.

Washington and Gist easily located and entered the dimly lit cabin, which was eerily dismal inside. The major was unsettled by a moment of quiet, and from ahead in the darkness came a voice. It was Aliquippa.

Her voice was aged and worn, yet to Washington it possessed a firmness that would have commanded respect from King George himself. Though he could only see her silhouette courtesy of the fires glowing outside, Washington did not hesitate to hand her gifts as a gesture of his goodwill. The first, a watch coat, was accepted and set aside. The second was a bottle of rum. Washington wrote that "[the] latter was thought much the best present of the two."

After dispensing the pleasantries, Aliquippa took on a serious tone. She leaned forward and addressed Washington, startling the major. Her skin was weathered, and wrinkles snaked aggressively across her face, no doubt from a lifetime of grave decision making. It was then that Washington saw the fire in her eyes, as youthful and passionate as ever, and he could only await her proclamation.

The young man stared into the eyes of the matriarch in front of him. He marveled at her poise, ambition and confidence. She had every quality that an effective leader should have: versatility, restraint, resolve and more. She was everything that he wanted to be.

Perhaps, though, Washington thought, it was her most staggering feature that she conveyed best in her old age: frailty. He was fixed on the elderly woman. He understood why she was called "Queen."

Aliquippa proceeded to talk of a way of life, the way that things once were, and the political and historic importance of the Valley of the Three Rivers to the Ohio Country and its peoples. She paused. Unsure whether to speak or remain silent, Washington began to mutter but was abruptly cut off.

The queen raised her voice, declaring forcefully that the British empire *must* take action against the emerging French presence in the region if balance was to be preserved. Washington knew what she was insinuating—her eyes said what her mouth didn't need to. Then, in the dark, dim chamber that the Seneca queen called home, she stated it plainly—and the words that she uttered would change the world forever: "The British must build a fort at the Forks of the Ohio."

Bibliography

Anderson, Fred. *The War that Made America: A Short History of the French and Indian War*. New York: Penguin Books, 2006.

Breen, T.H. *Tobacco Culture: The Mentality of the Great Tidewater Planters on the Eve of Revolution*. Princeton, NJ: Princeton University Press, 1987.

Ellis, Joseph J. *His Excellency: George Washington*. New York: Vintage, 2005.

Kent, Donald H. *The French Invasion of Western Pennsylvania*. Harrisburg: Pennsylvania Historical and Museum Commission, 1954.

Kopper, Kevin P. *The Journals of George Washington & Christopher Gist: Mission to Fort Le Boeuf*. Slippery Rock, PA: Slippery Rock University and Historic Harmony, 2009. This work is employed time and again. Not only is it a faithful compilation of both Washington's and Gist's writings, but Kevin Kopper's commentary on the geography of western Pennsylvania is also invaluable.

Sipe, C. Hale. *The Indian Chiefs of Pennsylvania*. Lewisburg, PA: Wennawoods Publishing, 2007.

Wallace, Paul A.W. *Historic Indian Paths of Pennsylvania*. Harrisburg: Pennsylvania Historical and Museum Commission, 1952.

INDEX

ABOUT THE AUTHOR

B rady J. Crytzer is the winner of both the 2010 Donald S. Kelly Award and 2010 Donna J. McKee Award for Outstanding Scholarship and Service in the Academic Discipline of History. He received his Master of Arts degree from Slippery Rock University of Pennsylvania.

Visit us at
www.historypress.net